Illustrated
Seamanship

Illustrated Seamanship

IVAR DEDEKAM

John Wiley & Sons, Ltd

Copyright © 2007   Ivar Dedekam

Published by   John Wiley & Sons Ltd, The Atrium, Southern Gate, Chichester,
West Sussex PO19 8SQ, England
Telephone (+44) 1243 779777

Email (for orders and customer service enquiries): cs-books@wiley.co.uk
Visit our Home Page on www.wileynautical.com

Other Wiley Editorial Offices

John Wiley & Sons Inc., 111 River Street, Hoboken, NJ 07030, USA

Jossey-Bass, 989 Market Street, San Francisco, CA 94103-1741, USA

Wiley-VCH Verlag GmbH, Boschstr. 12, D-69469 Weinheim, Germany

John Wiley & Sons Australia Ltd, 42 McDougall Street, Milton, Queensland 4064, Australia

John Wiley & Sons (Asia) Pte Ltd, 2 Clementi Loop #02-01, Jin Xing Distripark, Singapore 129809

John Wily & Sons Canada Ltd, 22 Worcester Road, Etobicoke, Ontario, Canada, M9W 1LI

Wiley also publishes its books in a variety of electronic formats. Some content that appears in print may not be available in electronic books.

Anniversary Logo Design: Richard J. Pacifico

Library of Congress Cataloging-in-Publication Data
Dedekam, Ivar.
  Illustrated seamanship / Ivar Dedekam.
     p. cm.
  Includes bibliographical references and index.
  ISBN 978-0-470-51220-3 (pbk. : alk. paper)
  1. Seamanship. 2. Yachting. I. Title.
  VK543.D3728 2007
  623.88--dc22

                                       2007013680

British Library Cataloguing in Publication Data
A catalogue record for this book is available from the British Library

ISBN-13: 978-0-470-51220-3

Typeset in 9/12 pt Swiss 721 BT by Laserwords Private Limited, Chennai, India
Printed and bound in Spain by Grafos
This book is printed on acid-free paper responsibly manufactured from sustainable forestry
in which at least two trees are planted for each one used for paper production.

Contents

Introduction

Today, yachts are often equipped with radar, GPS, chart plotters, electrical windlasses, autopilot, bow thrusters, etc. In addition, today's equipment has become much more reliable, making it possible to make long offshore passages without a basic knowledge of navigation and seamanship. However, as the coastguards in many countries can confirm, more and more yachts require assistance, even when they should be able to reach harbour on their own.

It is often only necessary to have a basic knowledge in order to voyage safely at sea. In this book you will be shown the *minimum* of techniques you should be familiar with, pertaining to rope handling, manoeuvring and anchoring, in order to make long passages with a reasonable degree of safety.

Although yacht gear is becoming more and more reliable, you can be almost sure that, sooner or later, it will fail or you will be out of electrical power to use it. Learning the traditional techniques may not only be necessary but is, in addition, both interesting and fun. Instead of waking up the entire harbour in an early morning hour with the noise of your bow thruster, you may, alternatively, use a spring line to get safely moored to or leave the pontoon.

Try practising the techniques and methods described in the book. Start in quiet conditions until you get the hang of it. You will then experience the joy of being able to handle your boat in this way, even if the boat is packed to the brim with modern equipment.

Good luck!

Ivar Dedekam

Ropework

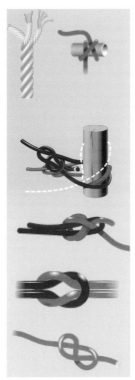
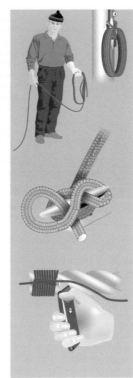

This chapter outlines the minimum level of knowledge of knots and hitches, whipping, splicing, etc. that you should have in order to make long passages. *Remember that it is better to know a few knots well than to half-know many*.

Take your time to learn these knots so you are able to tie them quickly. Preferably, you should be able to tie the knots with one hand and blindfolded! A good basic knowledge of ropework, knots and hitches may save both life and gear in dangerous situations.

THE BASICS

Ropes are made of short *fibres* that are spun into *yarns*, which are then made into flat or twisted *strands*. Finally,

the strands are spun or braided to make the finished rope (Figure 1.1). The two main types of rope are:

- **Laid rope:** three-strand rope (two- and four-strand ropes also exist) is made of strands twisted together in the opposite direction to that of the yarns, normally to the *right* (Z-laid), but sometimes to the *left* (S-laid).

- **Braided rope** is made in different ways. The yarns are normally braided to form a *sheath* covering an inner *core* of yarns, which may again be braided or lightly twisted together.

Materials

Natural fibres like *hemp, manila* and *sisal* were used for all rope until the 20th century. These fibres were derived from various plants and usually made into laid rope. Today, most rope is made from *synthetic fibres*.

The *fibre type* determines, to a large degree, the rope's properties:

- **Multifilament:** thin threads giving a supple/soft rope.
- **Film:** a flat, wide fibre used in cheap rope.
- **Monofilament:** a thick fibre giving a stiffer rope.

The material used can be divided into four groups:

- **Polyester** (Terylene) makes high quality rope made of *multifilament fibres*. The rope is supple (and remains supple), well protected against sunlight and sinks. A *high breaking strength* makes it suitable for anchor and mooring lines. Pre-stretched polyester rope, which gives minimum stretch, is used for sheets and halyards.

- **Polyamide** (Nylon) rope made of *multifilament fibres* is a high-stretch rope that is very much used in fishing and shipping. In common with polyester ropes, Nylon ropes have high abrasion resistance and don't float. In addition, they are very elastic, making them especially suitable for towing, mooring and climbing ropes where shock loads are introduced. Nylon rope is available in laid, braided and multibraided forms.

- **Polyethylene** rope made of *monofilament fibres* is smooth, with a relatively hard surface. This rope is used for heavy fishing gear due to its very high abrasion resistance.

- **Polypropylene** *fibres* make low-cost, all-purpose ropes. They are light and float, making them suitable as rescue or short mooring lines. However, the ropes have a low resistance to abrasion and sunlight. Polypropylene ropes come in a number of forms. Rope made from *film fibres* is inexpensive but should not be used on yachts, at least not where quality is necessary.

Note that *polyester, polyamide, polyethylene* and *polypropylene* are the correct names of the materials, while names like *Nylon, Terylene, Dacron*, etc. are the product names various companies use on products derived from these materials.

Aramid fibre (Kevlar) combines a very high breaking strength with a very low elasticity. A number of other fibres with names like *Vectran, Spectra* and *Dyneema* are light and often have higher breaking strengths than steel!

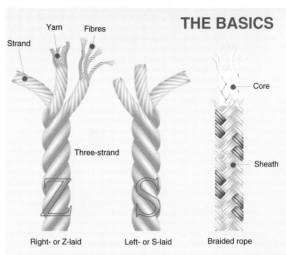

Three-strand

Right- or Z-laid   Left- or S-laid   Braided rope

Pre-stretched, braided polyester rope is much used for sheets and halyards. The rope has low elasticity and should not be used for mooring lines!

Braided, elastic Nylon rope is used for mooring and anchor lines. Three-stranded Nylon rope is also available (below).

Traditional *natural fibre ropes*, such as those made from *hemp* and *manila* are still available and are normally used on older, classic boats.

1

Kevlar (Aramid fibre): Higher breaking strength than steel and *very low stretch*. Easy to splice but should not be led around small-diameter sheaves.

Spectra (Dyneema): Breaking strength higher than steel and very high abrasion resistance.

These new fibres often have unique properties and you should therefore check thoroughly to see if they are suitable for your desired purpose. Ropes made from these new fibres often come with an *outer sheath* of polyester for easier handling.

Vectran also has a breaking strength higher than steel, has very low stretch and is hard-wearing.

2

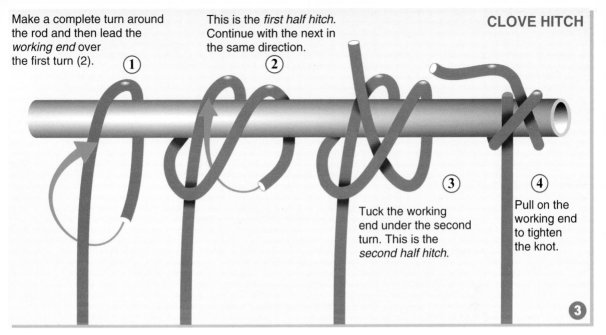

Make a complete turn around the rod and then lead the *working end* over the first turn (2). ①

This is the *first half hitch*. Continue with the next in the same direction. ②

③ Tuck the working end under the second turn. This is the *second half hitch*.

④ Pull on the working end to tighten the knot.

③

These ropes are expensive and are still used mostly on racing yachts (Figure 1.2).

CLOVE HITCH

The *clove hitch* is rather easy to make (Figure 1.3). You can add as many half hitches as you like, but always do the turns *in the same direction*. The hitch can be made mirrored and you may also make the turns in either direction relative to whatever you are making the knot on. You know that the knot is made properly when *the working end* and *the standing part* (the static part of the line) run in *parallel* in *opposite directions* under *the locking turn*. This knot is very basic and you should be able to tie it in both directions, starting the turn over or under the object on which you are making the knot.

The clove hitch (Figure 1.4) is one of the most commonly used knots. It is used in many variations for mooring lines and fenders. A *round turn with two half hitches* (6) should be used more often. Unlike the *bowline* (Figure 1.5), this knot may be untied *under load*. You make the clove hitch itself on the standing part of the line. You can make one or more complete turns around the pile in order to increase friction and to distribute the load better.

When you approach a pier, the fenders may be made fast with a clove hitch (5) and even made with a slip knot

(Figure 1.27). If the fenders are to be fixed for longer periods, it may be wiser to use a round turn with two half hitches (6). You can then be sure that the knot won't untie itself, thus avoiding losing a fender. The clove hitch alone may become untied if it is not tightened well from time to time.

BOWLINE

The *bowline* (Figure 1.5) is used when you want a fixed eye on, for example, a mooring line, or for tying sheets to a sail. The bowline is a very reliable knot that can be used for many purposes. *You should learn to make this knot blindfolded!* Many find the knot difficult to learn, although, like most things, it is only a matter of practice.

Imagine, for example, the small loop as a pond from which a sea snake (the working end) ascends and twirls itself around a tree (the standing part) and then slides back into the water following its body. (Make the first loop in exactly the same manner all the time. This makes the knot easier to learn).

The bowline can also be used to join two lines that are to be heavily loaded, where you want to be sure that you will be able to undo the knot afterwards. This is often a better solution than using a *double sheet bend* (Figure 1.8) or a *reef knot* (Figure 1.9). The latter should never

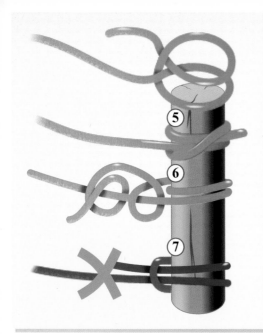

Both half hitches are made ready and are threaded on to the pile.

NB: The knot in this case may become stuck and also can't be untied under load.

A wrongly made clove hitch. You have made a *cow hitch* (or *lark's head*)!

A round turn with two half hitches, which can be untied under load, is a much better solution!

4

be used for such purposes! You can secure the bowline as shown (Figure 1.6) or make a stopper knot (Figure 1.10) if you want to be absolutely sure that it won't come undone (normally it does not). You may also make the bowline knot with a slip knot (Figure 1.6) in order to be able to undo it quickly. Always check that the working end protrudes an inch or two from the small loop to avoid the knot untying itself.

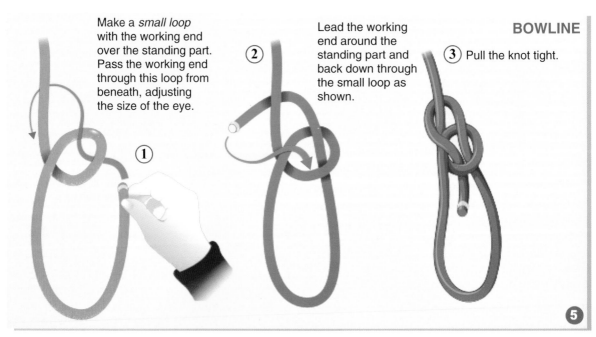

Make a *small loop* with the working end over the standing part. Pass the working end through this loop from beneath, adjusting the size of the eye.

①

② Lead the working end around the standing part and back down through the small loop as shown.

BOWLINE

③ Pull the knot tight.

5

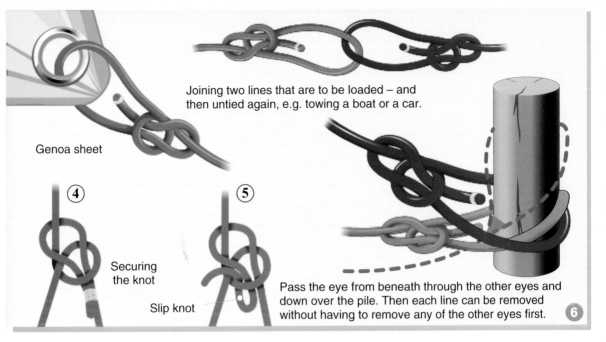

Joining two lines that are to be loaded – and then untied again, e.g. towing a boat or a car.

Genoa sheet

④

⑤

Securing the knot

Slip knot

Pass the eye from beneath through the other eyes and down over the pile. Then each line can be removed without having to remove any of the other eyes first. ⑥

SHEET BEND

The *sheet bend* (Figure 1.7) is normally used to join two ropes (Figure 1.8). If the ropes' diameters are unequal, a *double sheet bend* is used. The sheet bend is also used to attach ensigns to flag lines.

To make a sheet bend, fold the end of the first line (shown in blue in Figure 1.7) back on itself to form a loop if it doesn't have a fixed eye. Pass the working end of the other line (shown in red) through and around this loop (1), and then tuck it under itself but over the blue loop (2).

SHEET BEND

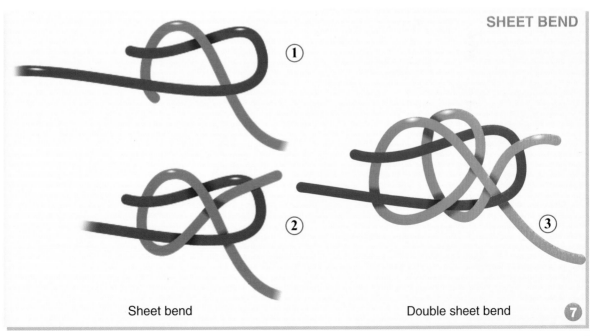

①

②

③

Sheet bend

Double sheet bend ⑦

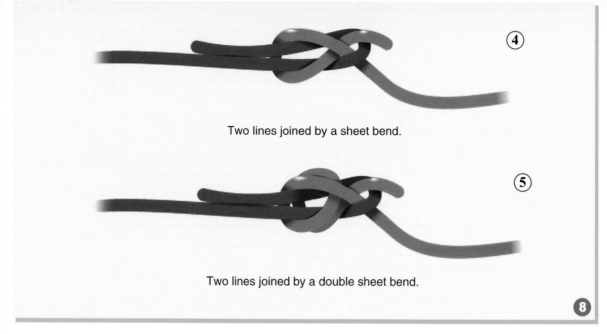

Two lines joined by a sheet bend.

Two lines joined by a double sheet bend.

④

⑤

⑧

You make a *double sheet bend* by leading the red working part once more around the loop and then taking it under itself but over the blue loop. Pull the knot tight. It is wise to use the double sheet bend most of the time, as it will almost never come loose.

The sheet bend can't be untied under load and it can be rather difficult to untie when relieved of the load. If you want to join two lines that will be heavily loaded, it is recommended that you use two bowlines tied 'inside each other' (Figure 1.6), as the bowline is far easier to untie when relieved of the load. If it isn't necessary to untie the ropes (permanent join), a double sheet bend can be a good solution.

REEF KNOT

The *reef knot* (or *square knot*) should only be used as a binding knot, for example to tie up sails on a boom. The well-known shoelace knot is actually a reef knot with two slip knots (Figure 1.9). The reef knot can't be untied under load but is easy to untie when relieved of the load. *It should never be used to join two lines that will be subject to any load, as it can easily come undone.* However, the knot can be used to join two lines of equal diameter that will be subject to very small loads.

STOPPER KNOTS

Stopper knots are used, for example, to prevent a sheet from slipping out of the sheet block on deck. The *figure of eight knot* (Figure 1.10) is the most commonly used stopper knot. The *double* (or multiple) *overhand knot* (2) is also much used, but this knot might be more difficult to undo than the figure of eight knot. It is *always important to make sure that a knot can be undone easily when desired, whilst at the same time ensuring that it can't open up accidentally.*

ROLLING HITCH

The *rolling hitch* is used to tie a line to a pole, wire or another line when you need a knot that won't slide when strain is applied sideways. Start by making two to five complete turns with the working end in the direction of the load, depending on how much friction you think you need (Figure 1.11). It may be necessary to remake the knot with more initial turns if it slides under load. *The rolling hitch is a very important knot to know; it can save you in many difficult or even dangerous situations.*

When, for example, a sheet under load is stuck on a winch, you may relieve the sheet by using a second line attached

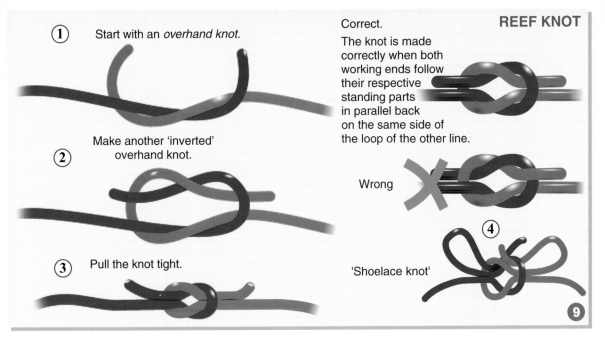

① Start with an *overhand knot.*

② Make another 'inverted' overhand knot.

③ Pull the knot tight.

Correct.

The knot is made correctly when both working ends follow their respective standing parts in parallel back on the same side of the loop of the other line.

Wrong

④ 'Shoelace knot'

⑨

with a rolling hitch (Figure 1.12) and leading to a second winch (2). Take in on the second winch until the sheet goes slack and may be relieved from the winch.

The rolling hitch is also very useful when you want to fix something to a wire or a smooth tube, for example fasten an ensign to a backstay. *Note that the hitch locks itself in the direction of the strain but may be moved quite easily in the opposite direction.* This can be used for a lot of purposes, for example to make movable steps by attaching loops to a shroud with rolling hitches. You

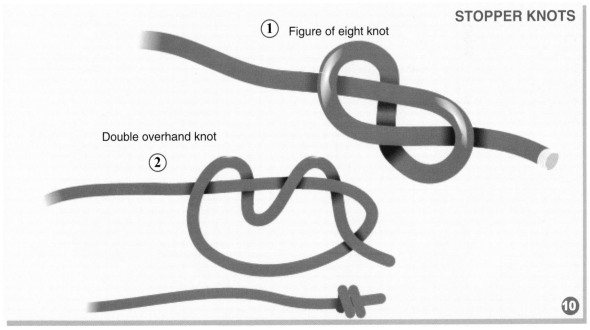

① Figure of eight knot

Double overhand knot

②

⑩

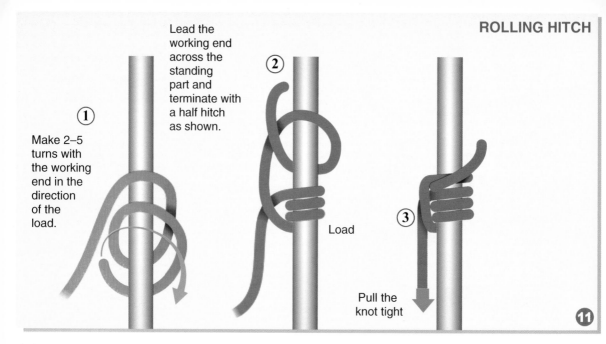

① Make 2–5 turns with the working end in the direction of the load.

② Lead the working end across the standing part and terminate with a half hitch as shown.

Load

③ Pull the knot tight

⑪

push the loop upwards and when your weight is on the loop, it locks to the wire, preventing the loop from sliding downwards. See also Figure 1.31 for another solution to this problem.

COILING ROPES

Right-laid rope needs to be coiled *clockwise* and given a right-hand twist in each turn in order to avoid *kinks* when the line runs out.

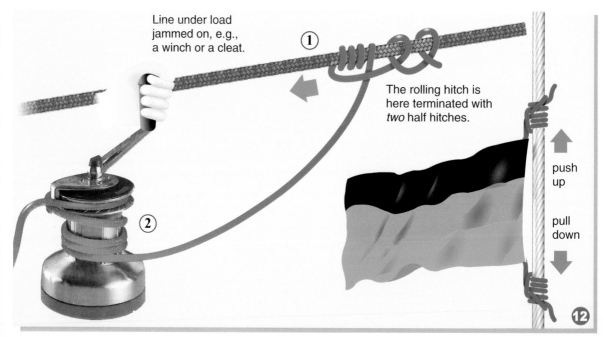

Line under load jammed on, e.g., a winch or a cleat.

①

②

The rolling hitch is here terminated with *two* half hitches.

push up

pull down

⑫

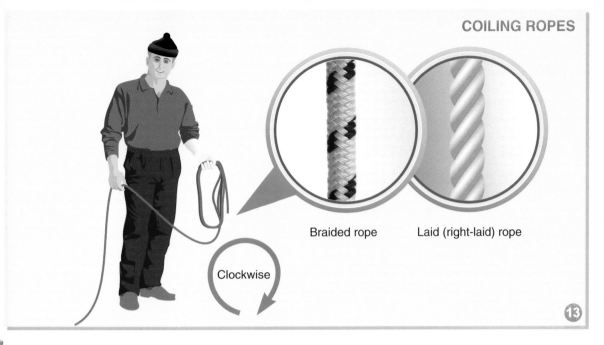

Braided rope   Laid (right-laid) rope

Clockwise

⑬

Halyards and *sheets* are now almost solely made of *braided rope*, which normally is coiled clockwise, although it really shouldn't be coiled at all! Braided rope that is coiled always risks having *kinks* when the line is running out. More often than not, braided rope is coiled in the same way as laid rope (Figure 1.13).

Many experts recommend coiling braided rope in figures of eight. Another, simpler, method is to lay loops

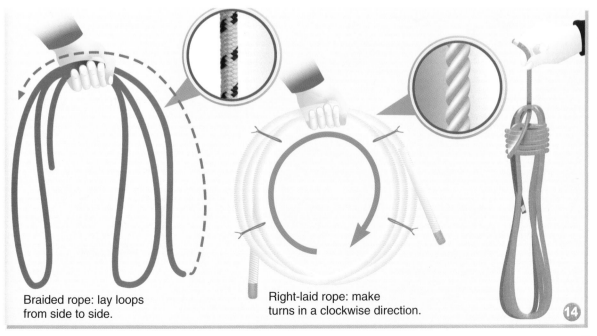

Braided rope: lay loops from side to side.

Right-laid rope: make turns in a clockwise direction.

⑭

from side to side (as shown in Figure 1.14), thus avoiding kinks.

When coiling *right-laid* (Z-laid) rope, you make the turns with one hand (normally the right hand) and lead them over to the other hand as they are made. This will, after some time, become an almost automatic movement. When you have finished coiling, you can secure the coil with thin laces (Figure 1.14), or you can terminate the coil with one of the techniques shown in Figures 1.15–1.18.

Left-laid rope, which is quite uncommon, should always be coiled *anticlockwise*.

Terminating the Coil

When you have coiled a line, grab the working end (Figure 1.15(1)) *on its way upwards* and turn it *around the coil* and *over* and *around itself*, creating *a lock*. You have to squeeze the loop (use your fingers) against the coil at A until the coil is locked with the next turn, which is to be made *downwards*. Make more turns *downwards* around the coil (2) and tuck the working end through the opening at the top of the coil (3). Pull everything tight as you push the loops around the coil upwards. Adjust the length of the working end according to whether the coil is to be suspended from a cleat or pushpit (4) or just stowed away.

A more common termination of a coil is shown in Figure 1.16. Take the working end *on its way downwards* (1) and lead it around the coil and over itself, making the lock. You have to squeeze the loop against the coil at A until it has been locked with the next turn. Make more turns *upwards* and make a loop on the working end, putting it through the opening at the top of the coil (2). Then wrap the loop over the top of the coil (3). Push the loops around the coil upwards and pull everything tight. You may also lead the working end through the loop, as shown by the arrow (4).

The methods described here are the most common. The method shown in Figure 1.15 is more difficult but is more stable over a period of time, especially in hard weather.

CLEATS

Making Fast on a Cleat

Keep the line, for example a halyard, tight and make a complete turn around the cleat (Figure 1.17). Then make *figures of eight* around the cleat (2 and 3). Terminate with a *half hitch* (4). Traditionally, half hitches were never used for fear of the line getting jammed under load. Instead, more figures of eight were laid on the cleat. Many cleats

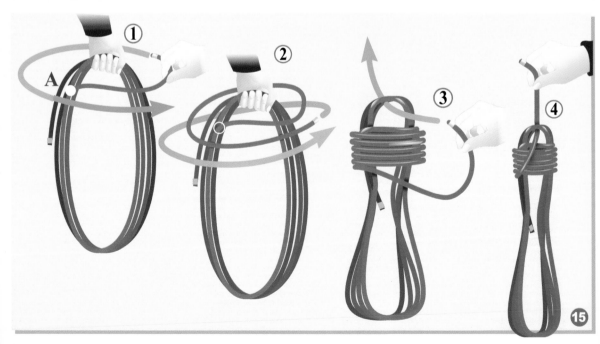

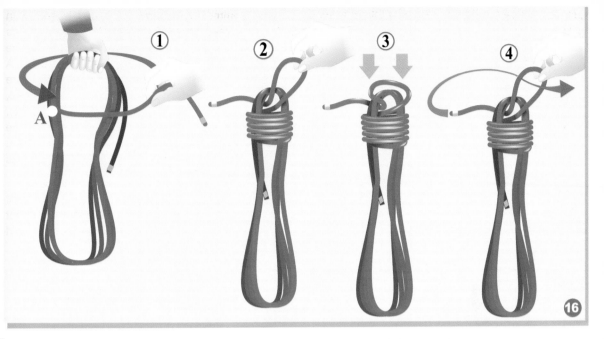

on modern yachts are too small for the lines used. Therefore, often only one figure of eight, terminated with a half hitch, is used. Sometimes there is even only room for one half turn before the figure of eight.

Stowing the Coil on a Cleat

Tighten the final half hitch and start coiling the rest of the line *from the cleat towards the free end* (Figure 1.18). Normally, the coil is made *clockwise*. Once you've finished coiling, use a hand to grab the fixed part of the line

MAKING FAST ON A CLEAT

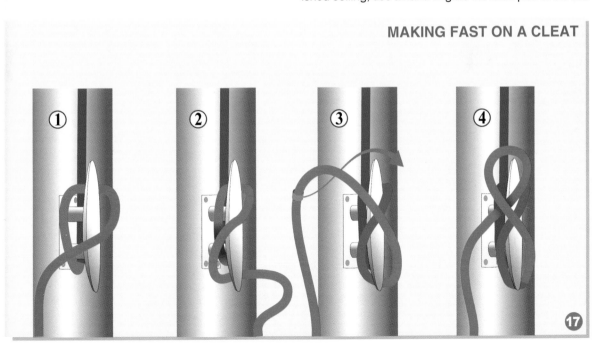

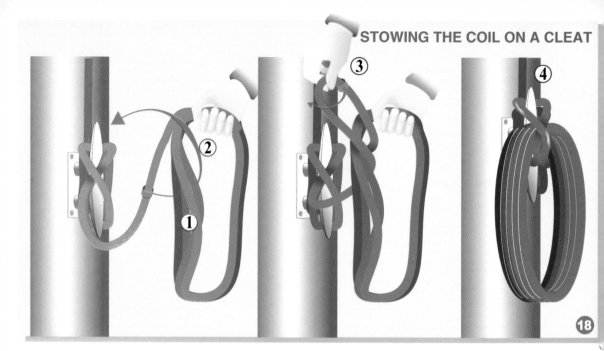

close to the cleat and pull a short loop through the coil (2). Wrap the loop by 180° (3) and hook it onto the cleat as shown (4). Note that you should get everything tighter than shown in the figure in order to secure the coil better. Therefore, you should grab the fixed part of the line as close as possible to the cleat and make the loop just big enough to get wrapped and hooked onto the cleat.

WHIPPING

The whipping shown in Figure 1.20 is easy to learn and can be used for many purposes. It can be used both on laid and braided lines as well as solid objects.

LASHINGS

There are three common types of lashing: *sheer*, *A-frame* and *square* lashings (Figure 1.22).

WINCH HANDLING

Always make a complete turn clockwise around the drum and then give the line a slight tug in order to hear the typical clicking sound that indicates that the line is laid in the correct direction (Figure 1.23). Then make two to three additional turns around the winch. If the winch is *self-tailing*, lead the line over the special *line guide* (3) and around and well into the *groove* (4). You can now use

both hands when winching in the line. If the winch is not of the self-tailing type, you have to use one hand to pull the tail of the line tight at all times when winching (5).

If you want to ease a loaded line slightly, you can almost *unscrew* the line with great precision by pressing the palm of the hand against the turns (Figure 1.24). (Needless to say, you must have enough turns around the winch and thus enough friction to be able to do this). To release the line quickly, for example when tacking a sailboat, flick the turns off the top of the winch in an *anti-clockwise* movement (7). If you want to add a turn when the line is under load, you should use both hands as shown (8). Be careful not to get your hand between the line and the winch (9). Keep in mind that the more turns around the winch, the easier it is to control the load, although the danger of *jamming* increases.

MAKING FAST ON A BOLLARD

When you want to make fast a chain on a bollard, you must first make two to three turns around the bollard (Figure 1.25). Make a bight that you put under the chain's standing part and then over the bollard (2). Ropes, especially synthetic ones, demand more turns in order to create enough friction (3). With enough around bollards and winches, you will be able to

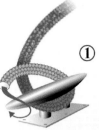

①

Make at least a *half turn*, preferably a whole one, around the cleat. Then begin making figures of eight.

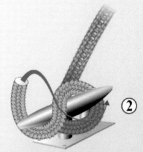

②

Make at least *two whole figures of eight*. If there is not enough room, settle on one or one and a half figures of eight.

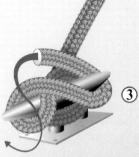

③

You may make as many figures of eight as the space allows.

④

We choose to finish off here by twisting the last half figure of eight by 90° ...

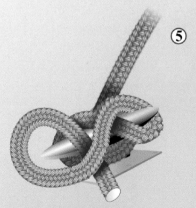

⑤

...and hook it onto the cleat as a *lock*.

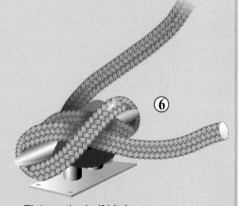

⑥

Tighten the half hitch.

 19

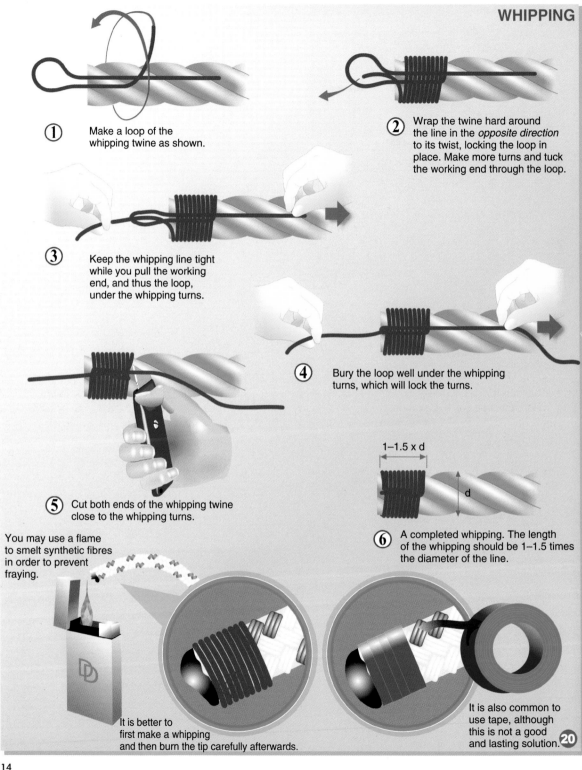

① Make a loop of the whipping twine as shown.

② Wrap the twine hard around the line in the *opposite direction* to its twist, locking the loop in place. Make more turns and tuck the working end through the loop.

③ Keep the whipping line tight while you pull the working end, and thus the loop, under the whipping turns.

④ Bury the loop well under the whipping turns, which will lock the turns.

⑤ Cut both ends of the whipping twine close to the whipping turns.

You may use a flame to smelt synthetic fibres in order to prevent fraying.

1–1.5 x d

d

⑥ A completed whipping. The length of the whipping should be 1–1.5 times the diameter of the line.

It is better to first make a whipping and then burn the tip carefully afterwards.

It is also common to use tape, although this is not a good and lasting solution. **20**

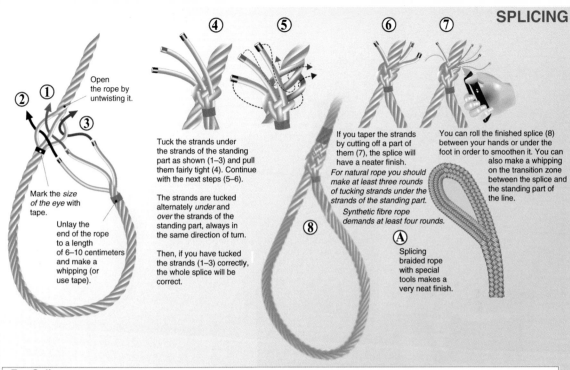

② ① ③

Open the rope by untwisting it.

Mark the *size of the eye* with tape.

Unlay the end of the rope to a length of 6–10 centimeters and make a whipping (or use tape).

Tuck the strands under the strands of the standing part as shown (1–3) and pull them fairly tight (4). Continue with the next steps (5–6).

The strands are tucked alternately *under* and *over* the strands of the standing part, always in the same direction of turn.

Then, if you have tucked the strands (1–3) correctly, the whole splice will be correct.

If you taper the strands by cutting off a part of them (7), the splice will have a neater finish.
For natural rope you should make at least three rounds of tucking strands under the strands of the standing part.
Synthetic fibre rope demands at least four rounds.

You can roll the finished splice (8) between your hands or under the foot in order to smoothen it. You can also make a whipping on the transition zone between the splice and the standing part of the line.

⑧

Ⓐ

Splicing braided rope with special tools makes a very neat finish.

Eye Splice

The *eye splice* is used to form a permanent loop at the end of a laid rope (normally three-stranded), for example on a mooring line. *Splicing braided rope* demands special tools and is not shown here. Such splices, however, will have a neat finish and you will hardly see the transition between the splice and the rope's standing part (A). *Note that an eye splice will reduce the rope's breaking strength by 20–30%.*

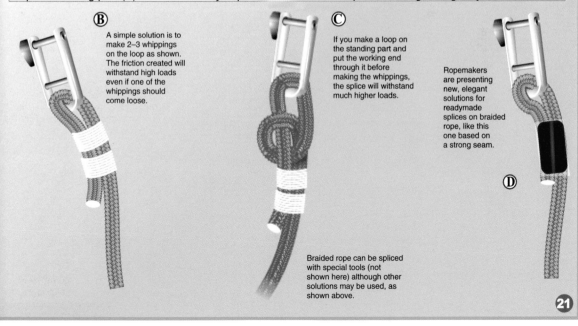

Ⓑ

A simple solution is to make 2–3 whippings on the loop as shown. The friction created will withstand high loads even if one of the whippings should come loose.

Ⓒ

If you make a loop on the standing part and put the working end through it before making the whippings, the splice will withstand much higher loads.

Ropemakers are presenting new, elegant solutions for readymade splices on braided rope, like this one based on a strong seam.

Ⓓ

Braided rope can be spliced with special tools (not shown here) although other solutions may be used, as shown above.

㉑

15

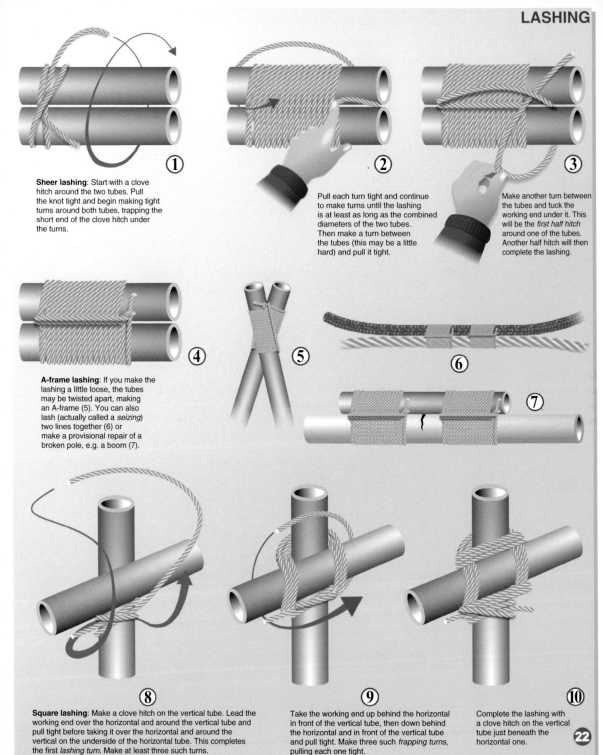

Sheer lashing: Start with a clove hitch around the two tubes. Pull the knot tight and begin making tight turns around both tubes, trapping the short end of the clove hitch under the turns.

Pull each turn tight and continue to make turns until the lashing is at least as long as the combined diameters of the two tubes. Then make a turn between the tubes (this may be a little hard) and pull it tight.

Make another turn between the tubes and tuck the working end under it. This will be the *first half hitch* around one of the tubes. Another half hitch will then complete the lashing.

A-frame lashing: If you make the lashing a little loose, the tubes may be twisted apart, making an A-frame (5). You can also lash (actually called a *seizing*) two lines together (6) or make a provisional repair of a broken pole, e.g. a boom (7).

Square lashing: Make a clove hitch on the vertical tube. Lead the working end over the horizontal and around the vertical tube and pull tight before taking it over the horizontal and around the vertical on the underside of the horizontal tube. This completes the first *lashing turn*. Make at least three such turns.

Take the working end up behind the horizontal in front of the vertical tube, then down behind the horizontal and in front of the vertical tube and pull tight. Make three such *frapping turns*, pulling each one tight.

Complete the lashing with a clove hitch on the vertical tube just beneath the horizontal one.

22

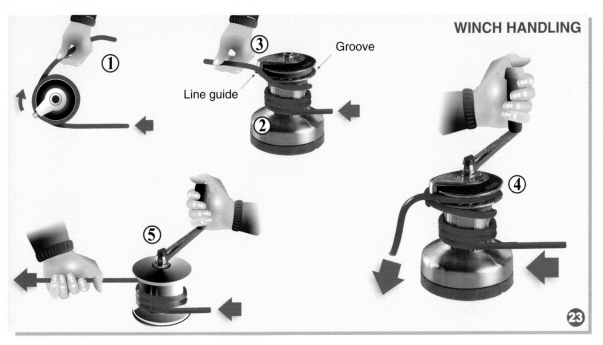

control big loads without any problems. The same goes for lines around cleats. *It is important that you understand this in order to be able to react quickly and automatically by adding a turn when you can't hold the load.*

SWIGGING (SWEATING)

If you want to tighten an already loaded line made fast on a cleat, you can pull the line at right angles and then let it go (Figure 1.26). This creates a little slack, which you quickly snatch around the cleat. You may do this

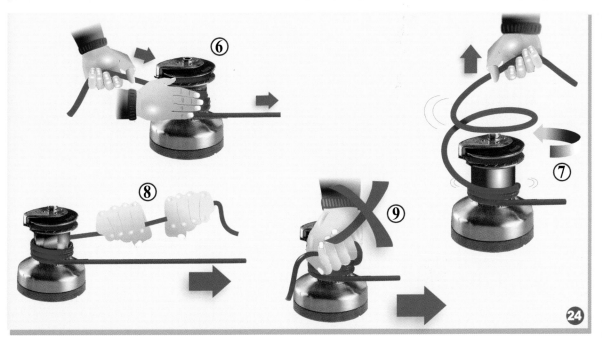

17

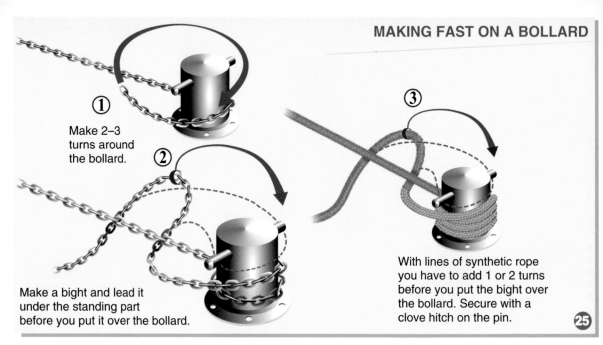

① Make 2–3 turns around the bollard.

② Make a bight and lead it under the standing part before you put it over the bollard.

③ With lines of synthetic rope you have to add 1 or 2 turns before you put the bight over the bollard. Secure with a clove hitch on the pin.

25

again to tighten the line even more. You can also use this technique to tighten halyards on a mast without the use of a winch. The reason for this is that when you pull the loaded line at right angles you will obtain a substantial power increase. This technique was used frequently on sailing ships, which did not have winches for many of the lines being handled.

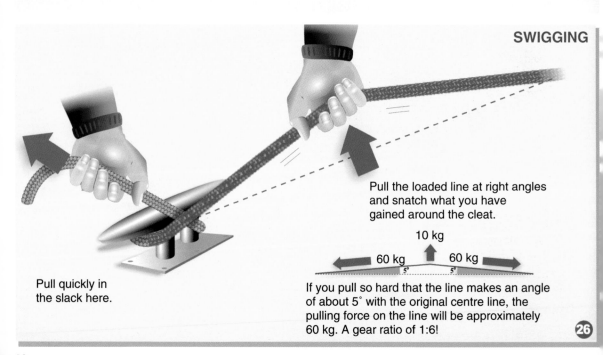

Pull the loaded line at right angles and snatch what you have gained around the cleat.

10 kg

60 kg ← 5° — 5° → 60 kg

Pull quickly in the slack here.

If you pull so hard that the line makes an angle of about 5° with the original centre line, the pulling force on the line will be approximately 60 kg. A gear ratio of 1:6!

26

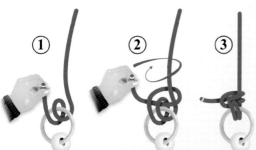

① ② ③

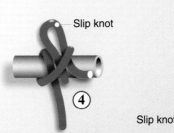

Slip knot

④

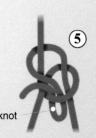

⑤

Slip knot

Slip knot

⑥

The *anchor bend* or *fisherman's bend* is a variation on a round turn with two half hitches (Figure 1.4). It is used to tie a rope directly to an anchor or mooring when you want to be sure that the knot won'tcome untied.

Making a bowline quickly might be a very useful skill to possess. You may avoid dangerous situations by first preparing and then quickly making the knot.

Example: A bowline may be made ready (Step 1–3) before jumping ashore. You then lead the working end through, e.g. a mooring ring, adjust the size of the loop (Step 4) and complete the knot with a short tug on the standing part (Step 5–6).

Most knots may be completed with a slip knot in order to be able to untie the knot quickly, e.g. clove hitch (Step 4), bowline (Step 5) and sheet bend (Step 6).

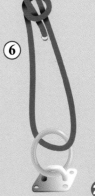

①
Hold the line as shown and twist your hand clockwise through 180°.

②
Put your fingers through the loop which will now be formed and grab hold of the standing part.

③
Pull the standing part through the loop.

④
Put the working end through the mooring ring and lead it up through the loop from below.

⑤
Double the working end back and hold it against itself. Give the standing part a short tug and the bowline will be completed (6). (Sometimes you have to help the locking turn to find its right position).

⑥

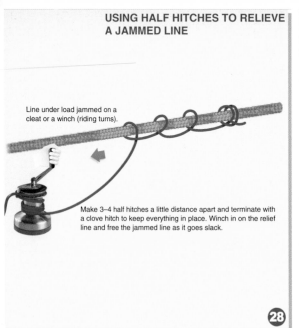

Line under load jammed on a
cleat or a winch (riding turns).

Make 3–4 half hitches a little distance apart and terminate with
a clove hitch to keep everything in place. Winch in on the relief
line and free the jammed line as it goes slack.

28

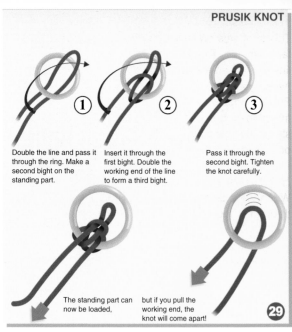

① Double the line and pass it
through the ring. Make a
second bight on the
standing part.

② Insert it through the
first bight. Double the
working end of the line
to form a third bight.

③ Pass it through the
second bight. Tighten
the knot carefully.

The standing part can
now be loaded,

but if you pull the
working end, the
knot will come apart!

29

Using Half Hitches to Relieve a Jammed Line

Instead of using the rolling hitch when a line is jammed, as shown in the example in Figure 1.12, several half hitches a little distance apart can do the trick (Figure 1.28). Both of these methods can also be used to relieve a jammed chain. It is wise to try out these techniques before you actually need to use them.

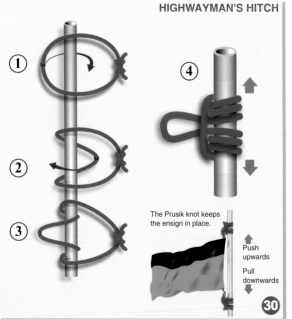

①
②
③
④

The Prusik knot keeps
the ensign in place.

Push
upwards

Pull
downwards

30

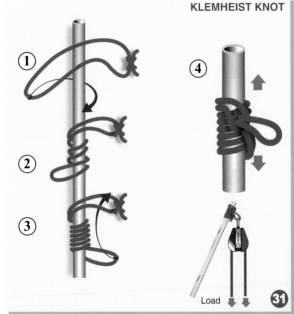

①
②
③
④

Load

31

The Prusik Knot

This knot was created by Carl Prusik for use in mountain climbing. To make the knot, first make a loop on a line with a diameter less than half the diameter of the line (wire, tube) to which you want to fasten it (Figure 1.29). Put the loop around the line and 'through itself'. Repeat this at least twice and pull the knot tight. Now the knot should be able to withstand loads in both directions without slipping.

Highwayman's Hitch

When, for example, you don't want to pass a slip line through a mooring ring for fear of it getting jammed, the highwayman's hitch could be useful (Figure 1.30). A short pull on the unloaded end of the line will quickly release the hitch (although this makes it quite easy to release accidentally).

The Klemheist Knot

A useful variation on the Prusik knot is the Klemheist knot (Figure 1.31). Turn the loop tightly and evenly around the wire (or rope) and pull it tight. Give it a test to make sure it can hold the intended load. If it slips, you have to add turns. Two such knots around a halyard can be used to climb a mast by pushing the knots upwards alternately.

Boat Handling

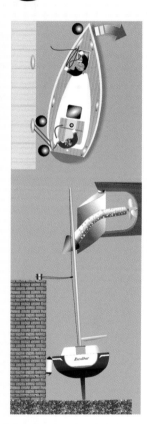

Basic techniques for manoeuvring a yacht in harbours and confined spaces under various wind and sea conditions are described in this chapter. In addition, you are shown how to approach and moor safely to berths, pontoons, buoys and piles and also how to leave them properly. Using springs to facilitate and secure manoeuvring is also described thoroughly.

Even if bow thrusters and increased engine power make it easier to manoeuvre, it is vital to know the basic techniques in order to handle your boat safely in confined spaces.

THE BASICS

It is important to understand that a boat cannot be handled in the same way as a car. It is more like handling a car on a slippery surface. We will look at the reasons for this on the next few pages. Suffice it to say that you must, at all times, take into consideration the various factors shown in Figure 2.1 when manoeuvring. The hull shape and an eventual rig may have a great impact on a boat's handling characteristics, although you can't alter these much when manoeuvring. *This makes it crucial that you know how your yacht will handle under various*

The most important factors influencing a boat's motion through the water:

- ☐ **Hull shape** (together with an eventual rig)
- ☐ **Slipstream and paddle effect from the propeller**
- ☐ **Rudder shape and size**
- ☐ **Wind forces and waves**
- ☐ **Currents** (both tidal and wind-driven currents)

❶

conditions. Currents also have an effect, and we will look at these in more detail later.

Terms and Expressions

It is important to realise that there are differences between the language we use and understand on shore and the language we use at sea. For example, the terms *starboard* and *port side* are *not* the same as right and left, but refer to the *two halves* of a boat (Figure 2.2). Regardless of which direction you are facing, the starboard and port side of the boat will be the same. This enables you to describe precisely where on a boat, or

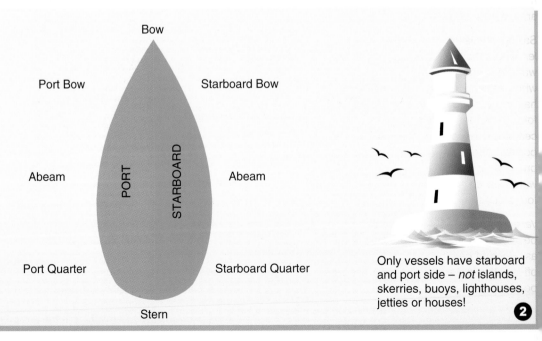

Only vessels have starboard and port side – *not* islands, skerries, buoys, lighthouses, jetties or houses!

❷

relative to it, something is located or something takes place. We describe, for example, the *port navigation light* or we say that something may *pass the boat to starboard* or *port.* Similarly, 'reversing' is not a correct seafaring term. However, maritime language is becoming more and more similar to the language used ashore.

THE PROPELLER

Normally, the propeller rotates *clockwise* as viewed from astern when the boat is going forwards. This is known as a *right-handed propeller*. Some propellers rotate *anticlockwise* when the boat is driven forwards and are known as *left-handed propellers*. When the propeller rotates in forward, it throws out a *slipstream* astern. This causes a counter force (reaction) which drives the boat forwards (Figure 2.3). In addition, the propeller tries to *paddle across sideways* in the direction it is turning. A right-handed propeller will pull the stern to starboard when going ahead and to port when going astern. In order to understand the paddle effect better, imagine that the propeller touches the seabed and rolls sideways, rather like a wheel. This is known as the *paddlewheel effect* and is very important in the handling of the boat (Figure 2.3). The effect is greater with large, slowly rotating propellers and is more marked when going astern.

Propellers come in many shapes, with both fixed and movable blades. Propellers with two, three or four blades are the most common.

Sailing yachts are often equipped with a *folding propeller*, where the blades are hinged at the boss so that the water pressure pushes them back in line with the shaft when sailing with the engine stopped. (Often the gear has to be put in reverse in order to get the blades to fold). When the engine is started and the shaft rotates, centrifugal forces pull the blades out into their driving position and the boat is pushed forwards. The folding propeller is less efficient going astern than a propeller with fixed blades. Folding propellers come with two to four blades.

Variable-pitch propellers have movable blades that can be twisted in the boss to vary the pitch. This may be seen as a kind of gearbox. A fine pitch is used when starting off and this is then gradually coarsened to increase the boat's speed.

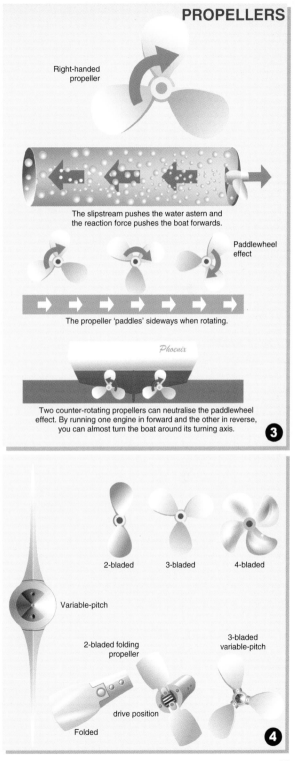

PROPELLERS

Right-handed propeller

The slipstream pushes the water astern and the reaction force pushes the boat forwards.

Paddlewheel effect

The propeller 'paddles' sideways when rotating.

Phoenix

Two counter-rotating propellers can neutralise the paddlewheel effect. By running one engine in forward and the other in reverse, you can almost turn the boat around its turning axis. **3**

2-bladed   3-bladed   4-bladed

Variable-pitch

2-bladed folding propeller

3-bladed variable-pitch

drive position

Folded   **4**

The *feathering propeller* is a type of variable-pitch propeller often fitted to sailing yachts to reduce drag when sailing. It is normally two-bladed so it can be aligned with the sternpost. It can be set to feather automatically when sailing. It is as efficient as a fixed-blade propeller when going astern.

There are also variable-pitch propellers (especially suited for sailing yachts) where the blades are *automatically* set to minimise drag when sailing and where the pitch can be adjusted to obtain the maximum performance of the boat. When the engine is started, the shaft will twist the blades into the *preset* drive position. When going astern, the rotation of the shaft twists the blades as in ahead, but this time in the opposite direction, so that the *leading edge* of the blades cuts the water (contrary to fixed and folding propellers). The pitch in reverse is the same as in ahead, which often makes the efficiency of the propeller *greater* in reverse than a fixed-blade propeller.

Two propellers can make manoeuvring easier, especially if both propellers are located in front of their proper rudders. They normally rotate in opposite directions and therefore, theoretically, neutralise the paddlewheel effect (Figure 2.3). But in reality, this effect is never exactly the same for both propellers, especially if the two propellers are operated independently. But you can then run one propeller in ahead and the other in reverse, thus reducing the turning radius significantly.

THE RUDDER

When the *rudder* is turned, the slipstream from the propeller and/or the water flow caused by the boat's speed through the water will be deflected. This creates a *reaction force* on the rudder (Figure 2.5) that will push the stern sideways. In astern, the rudder isn't as efficient as in ahead because the water flow deflected by the rudder is not as strong and is more turbulent when the water is pushed ahead (Figure 2.6). Therefore, the boat can first be steered astern in a controlled manner when the speed through the water has reached what is known as *steering speed*.

The rudder can even turn the boat when the engine is stopped. Here, there must be a current that causes water to flow past the rudder. Otherwise, the boat has to

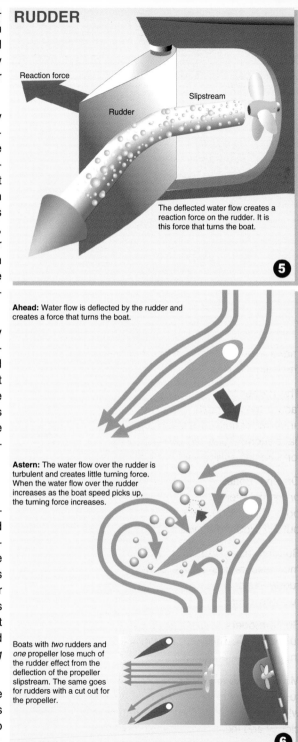

RUDDER

Reaction force

Slipstream

Rudder

The deflected water flow creates a reaction force on the rudder. It is this force that turns the boat.

5

Ahead: Water flow is deflected by the rudder and creates a force that turns the boat.

Astern: The water flow over the rudder is turbulent and creates little turning force. When the water flow over the rudder increases as the boat speed picks up, the turning force increases.

Boats with *two* rudders and *one* propeller lose much of the rudder effect from the deflection of the propeller slipstream. The same goes for rudders with a cut out for the propeller.

6

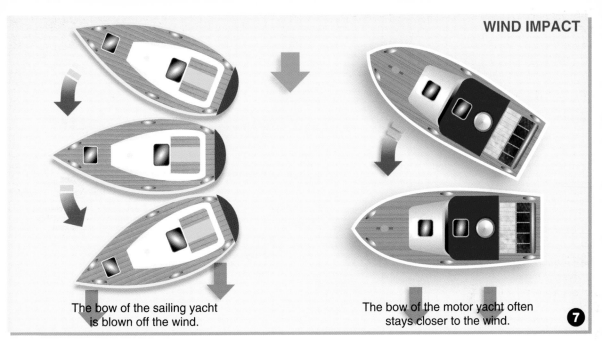

The bow of the sailing yacht is blown off the wind.

The bow of the motor yacht often stays closer to the wind.

7

make speed through the water so the rudder can deflect the water flow.

The rudder tries to push the boat's stern sideways. In fact, it tries to push the whole boat sideways, but the underwater hull, depending on its form, will resist this. A flat-bottomed boat will be pushed more sideways than a long-keeled sailing yacht with a deep hull.

On small boats, the rudder can be used as an *emergency brake* by alternately giving full helm to starboard and port. This will not cause any significant course change but the rudder *drag* will decrease boat speed.

Rudders hinged on a fin or the hull itself are normally more secure than *spade rudders*, which are fixed to the rudder stock and only supported by a bearing above the rudders' overside.

Some rudders have a part of the surface forward of the rudder stock. These are known as *balanced rudders* and they make steering easier.

Most rudders are equipped with *stoppers* that limit the rudder angle to about 40°. The rudder will create big whirls at greater angles, thus reducing the rudder efficiency and increasing drag significantly.

Most beginners use too much helm. It is better to use small, frequent rudder corrections than fewer, bigger ones.

WIND IMPACT

When the boat is not making its way through the water and the engine is in neutral, the bow of a sailing yacht will normally be blown off the wind and end up with the wind on *the quarter* (Figure 2.7). This happens because the hull is not as deep forward as aft and because the mast is located relatively far forward. The hull depth of motor yachts is often more evenly distributed and they tend to end up with the wind *abeam* (Figure 2.7).

Wind impact comes in addition to rudder and propeller forces and with great differences between various types of boat. *Try out your own boat and observe carefully how it performs under various wind conditions.*

The Influence of the Hull Shape

Some boats have so much windage aft that the bow will always tend to seek into the wind. Others have so much windage forward that in strong winds it will almost be impossible to get the bow close to the wind when the boat speed is low.

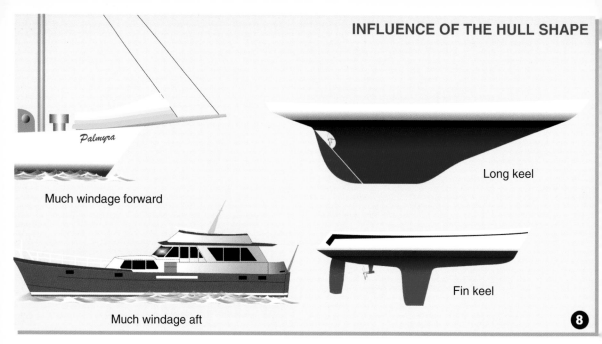

Palmyra

Much windage forward

Much windage aft

Long keel

Fin keel

8

The *underwater hull* has a great influence on a boat's manoeuvring capability. A modern fin-keeled sailing yacht has a much smaller turning circle than a long-keeled yacht. The fin-keeled yacht will react more quickly on the helm and is easier to handle when manoeuvring in confined spaces (Figure 2.8).

THE BOAT'S TURNING CURVE

When the boat goes straight ahead (Figure 2.9) and you put the helm over, the boat will begin to turn around a point known as the *turning point*. At the same time, this point moves along a more or less circular *turning curve*

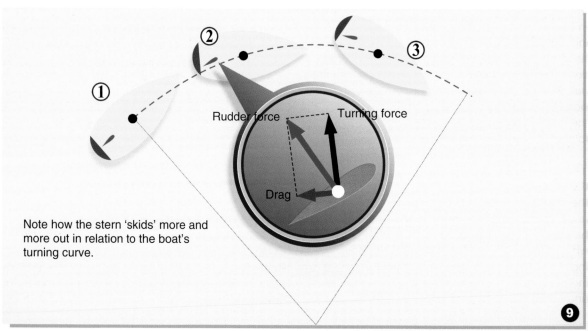

① ② ③

Rudder force

Turning force

Drag

Note how the stern 'skids' more and more out in relation to the boat's turning curve.

9

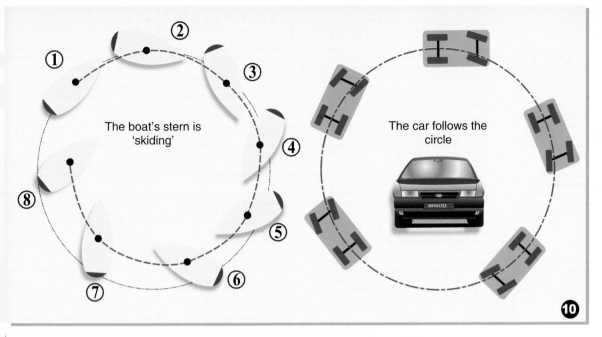

The boat's stern is 'skiding'

The car follows the circle

with decreasing radius. The movement of the boat is composed of a *forward motion*, a *sideways drift* and *turning* around the turning point. This is the reason why a boat's stern will be 'skidding' in the turn. *Imagine the boat as a car on a slippery surface when you are turning!*

It is important to understand that there are big differences in how various types of boat behave when manoeuvring, especially in confined spaces. When you put the helm over, the boat will turn around a point, the location of which is decided by the shape of the *underwater hull*. This point is located forward of amidships for most boats. This causes the stern of the boat to 'skid' when the boat is turning, contrary to a car where the aft end follows the turning circle (Figure 2.10).

The Wind's Influence on the Turning Curve

If you turn the boat *away from* the wind, the wind helps the boat to turn. You can then reduce the engine power and let the wind do the job (Figure 2.11). On the other hand, when you have to turn up *against* the wind, the wind will try to blow the bow of the boat to *leeward*, making the turning curve larger. It may then be necessary to increase engine power in order to counteract the wind and reduce the turning curve (Figure 2.11).

GOING ASTERN

To go astern *against the wind* is normally relatively easy. The wind blows the bow *to leeward* all the time and the boat acts almost as a wind vane (Figure 2.12).

Going astern to *leeward* (in the same direction as the wind blows) is much more complicated, as the bow will normally be blown to either side (Figure 2.12). Combined with the propeller's *paddlewheel effect*, the bow may suddenly bear away and create problems. Going astern to leeward therefore demands full concentration from the helmsman and adequate steering speed.

If, for some reason, you have to lie idle waiting for, for example, a bridge or a lock to open, it may be a good idea to go slowly astern *against the wind*. Apply just enough power to counteract the wind. In fresh wind conditions this technique can save you a lot of manoeuvring.

GETTING TO KNOW YOUR BOAT

Try out the engine controls when your boat is securely moored in a berth. Put the engine in forward, then in neutral and lastly in astern and vary the engine revs to get a feel for the controls. To find out which way the propeller rotates, put the engine in astern and watch the slipstream, as shown in Figure 2.13 (or look directly at

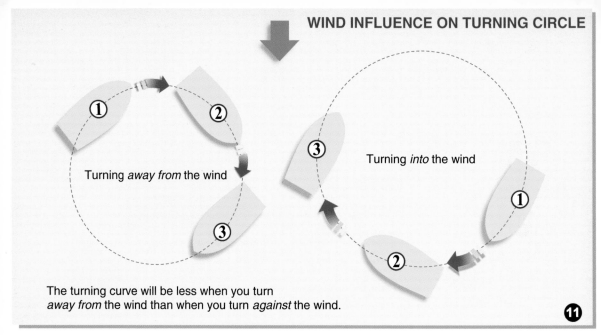

WIND INFLUENCE ON TURNING CIRCLE

Turning *away from* the wind

Turning *into* the wind

The turning curve will be less when you turn
away from the wind than when you turn *against* the wind.

11

the shaft if possible). Get used to looking forward and not down on the controls when manoeuvring. Also, get used to standing up so you have the best view of the situation.

Go out in open waters or somewhere you may train without being disturbed and find out how the boat behaves in different situations. You will then get to know your boat better in a safe way, which is well worth the effort. This is done by all too few yachtsmen! You can use buoys or fenders with a weight on the end of a line as markers. Use these markers to simulate

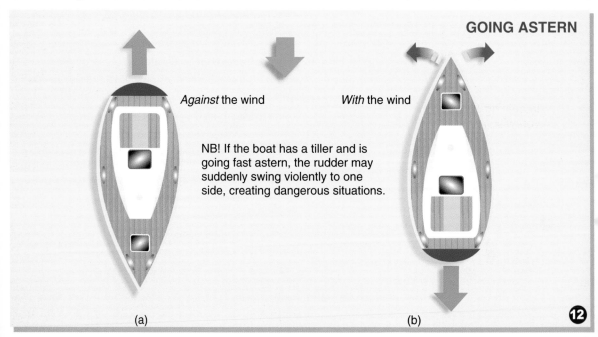

GOING ASTERN

Against the wind

With the wind

NB! If the boat has a tiller and is going fast astern, the rudder may suddenly swing violently to one side, creating dangerous situations.

(a)

(b)

12

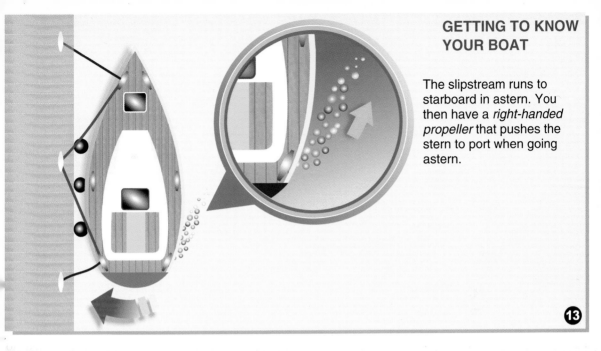

The slipstream runs to starboard in astern. You then have a *right-handed propeller* that pushes the stern to port when going astern.

13

a berth or a quay (Figure 2.14) in order to learn to estimate angles and distances. It is especially important to know the distance necessary to stop your boat completely. Note how the boat behaves during vari- ous sea and wind conditions and how fast it drifts due to wind and current. *Always be aware of other boats and people and remember that the collision regulations apply.*

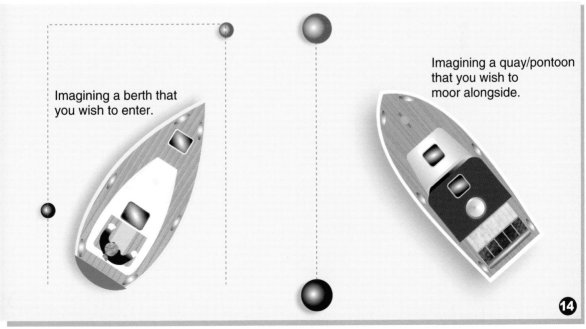

Imagining a berth that you wish to enter.

Imagining a quay/pontoon that you wish to moor alongside.

14

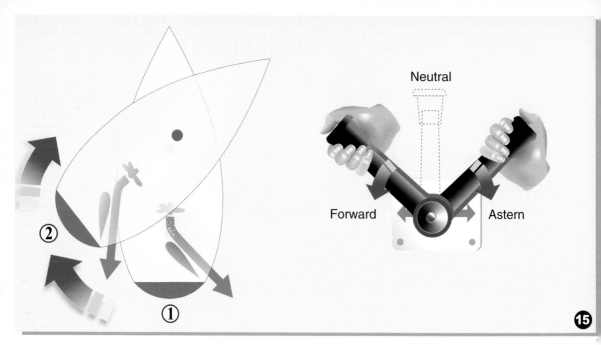

TURNING THE BOAT IN CONFINED SPACES

Many boats can be turned through 180° in little more than a boat length in light conditions, by applying short, strong *bursts* of power alternately *forward* and *astern* with the *rudder in a fixed position*. From position (1) in Figure 2.15 when the boat is not moving, put the helm over and give full throttle in forward. The bow will now *turn to starboard* in this example. As soon as the boat starts to *move forwards*, put the engine control in neutral for one to two seconds and then give full throttle astern (2) until the boat just starts to move astern.

As soon as the boat begins to move *astern* in position (2), put the engine in neutral again for one to two seconds and then give full throttle *forward*. When the boat starts to move forwards, apply full throttle *astern* until it stops (Figure 2.16, position (3)). Continue in the same manner until you have turned the boat (4). *It is important to keep the tiller or wheel in a fixed position during the turning manoeuvre. The boat will not steer in the short periods in astern anyway.*

Note that this technique only works well on boats where the propeller is located relatively close *forward* of the rudder, so that the slipstream in forward hits the rudder. It is the deflection of the slipstream that turns the boat.

Engine Handling

Don't be afraid of giving *full throttle* from a standstill. It always takes some time before the boat starts to move forwards. The rudder, however, gets the full slipstream at once and starts to push the stern sideways. You must *exploit this as much as possible* before the boat starts to move forwards. Then put the engine control quickly in neutral for one to two seconds. This is done to save the gearbox from unnecessary wear. Now quickly give full throttle astern in order to stop any forward movement (Figure 2.17). *It is during these short periods in forward that most of the process of turning the boat takes place.*

In astern, the rudder doesn't have any impact when manoeuvring in this manner (Figure 2.18). Therefore, it is of little avail to turn the rudder in the short moments with the engine in astern. It is when the boat first gains some speed in astern that the increased water flow over the rudder makes it work better. The paddlewheel effect, however, is more marked in astern than in forward. Therefore, it is better to make a 180° turn to *starboard* when your boat has a *right-handed propeller*.

You should test your boat in quiet conditions to see how it handles during a 180° turn. In some boats, the engine

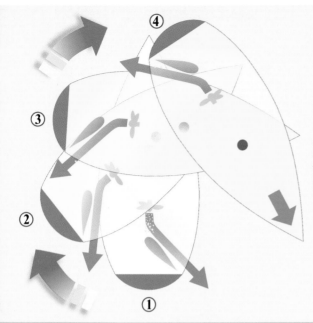

180° turn to starboard:

A *right-handed propeller* will here pull the stern to port when going astern and facilitate the manoeuvre. A turn to port will, in this case, be more difficult.

16

controls are located in such a manner that you have to bend down, thus losing your viewpoint when manoeuvring. This is *not recommended*, and some yachtsmen therefore use their feet to operate the controls. It is better to have the controls moved.

ENTERING AND LEAVING A BERTH

Leaving a Berth Going Astern
Always note the *wind direction* before you leave a berth. Remember that the boat first obtains an adequate

ENGINE HANDLING

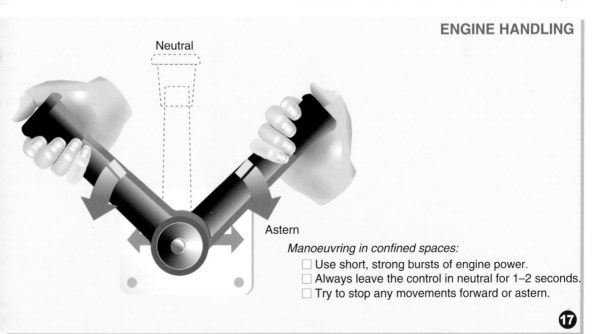

Neutral

Astern

Manoeuvring in confined spaces:
☐ Use short, strong bursts of engine power.
☐ Always leave the control in neutral for 1–2 seconds.
☐ Try to stop any movements forward or astern.

17

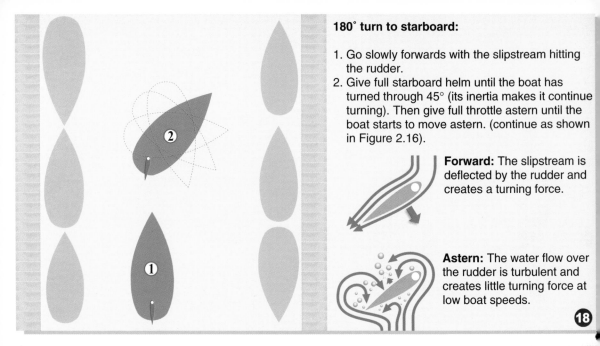

180° turn to starboard:

1. Go slowly forwards with the slipstream hitting the rudder.
2. Give full starboard helm until the boat has turned through 45° (its inertia makes it continue turning). Then give full throttle astern until the boat starts to move astern. (continue as shown in Figure 2.16).

Forward: The slipstream is deflected by the rudder and creates a turning force.

Astern: The water flow over the rudder is turbulent and creates little turning force at low boat speeds.

18

steering speed after it has moved astern *some boat lengths*. Wind in from *starboard* doesn't pose any problem here (Figure 2.19). Go slowly astern, letting the wind blow the bow to leeward until it is clear of the berth.

Wind in from *port* (Figure 2.20) will blow the bow in the 'wrong' direction and you have to use the technique shown in Figures 2.15 and 2.16 in order to get the bow into the wind (Figure 2.21). Or you may need to use a

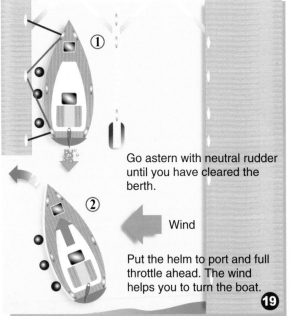

Go astern with neutral rudder until you have cleared the berth.

Wind

Put the helm to port and full throttle ahead. The wind helps you to turn the boat.

19

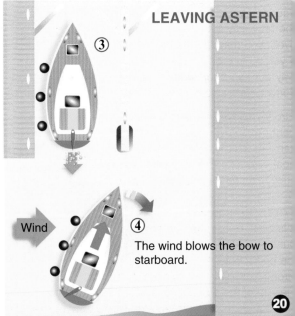

LEAVING ASTERN

Wind

The wind blows the bow to starboard.

20

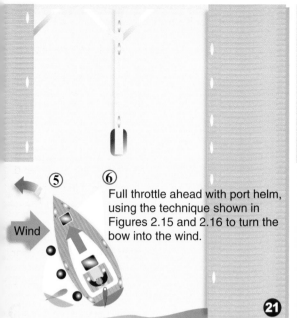

⑤ ⑥ Full throttle ahead with port helm, using the technique shown in Figures 2.15 and 2.16 to turn the bow into the wind.

Wind

㉑

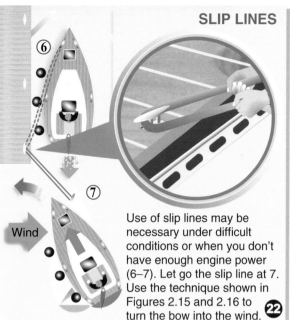

⑦ Use of slip lines may be necessary under difficult conditions or when you don't have enough engine power (6–7). Let go the slip line at 7. Use the technique shown in Figures 2.15 and 2.16 to turn the bow into the wind. ㉒

Wind

slip line to prevent the bow from blowing too far to starboard (see Figure 2.22).

Slip Lines

Wind in from the *port side* will normally blow the bow to starboard (Figure 2.20). A right-handed propeller will push the stern to port, making everything more difficult. You therefore have to use engine power in order to get the bow into the wind and clear the pontoon. Alternatively, you may use a *slip line*, as shown in Figure 2.22. If you have problems, it is possible *to go astern all the way* out into open water – especially when the wind is coming from astern.

Strong headwinds may blow the bow to *either side* in the berth. To be safe, you can rig one or more slip lines. You can also set a crew member ashore or onboard another boat with a line. When you have cleared the berth, the crew member can be picked up again in a safer spot.

Entering a Berth

It is wise to give the pontoon a wide berth (pardon the pun!) in order to steer more easily into the middle of the berth. Enter the berth slowly and make a short and strong kick astern when you are one to two metres from the end of the berth. With no wind you can glide slowly into the berth with the engine in neutral. But you are always more in control with *slipstream over the rudder*, especially when wind or current affects the boat (Figures 2.23 and 2.24). Note that when you make a kick astern in the berth, the stern will be pushed more or less to either side due to the paddlewheel effect.

Wind on the beam makes it necessary either to make a tighter turn or give the pontoon a wider berth while entering, as the boat will be blown sideways (Figures 2.25 and 2.26). Only trial and error can give you the necessary experience to control the boat. If you worry about going astern too late, you may try small 'test-kicks' astern when the boat *has a straight course* into the berth. After some time, you will get a feel for how strong the kicks astern need be in order to stop the boat. Never go so hard astern that the boat starts to *move astern*! Look sideways at the pontoon when you make your kick astern; you will then see more easily when the speed diminishes and the boat has made a complete stop.

COMING ALONGSIDE

Always make *all mooring lines* ready and put out enough fenders (an extra fender in the bow) when approaching a quay. Approach at an angle of 20–30° (Figure 2.27), before turning parallel to the quay (2). Make a short, strong kick astern to stop the boat (3). Set ashore a crew member or members to make fast the mooring lines.

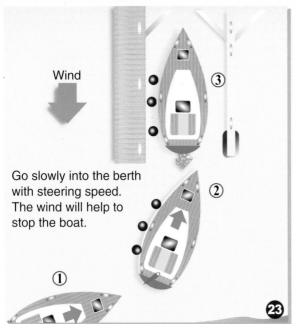

Wind

Go slowly into the berth with steering speed. The wind will help to stop the boat.

③
②
①

23

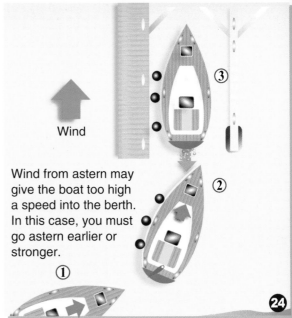

Wind

Wind from astern may give the boat too high a speed into the berth. In this case, you must go astern earlier or stronger.

③
②
①

24

The crew should stand at the 'beamiest' part of the boat – close to the shrouds on sailing yachts. *It is often wise to first make a circuit to have a look at the conditions before closing in on the quay. This also gives you time to check once more that all the mooring lines and fenders are ready and correctly located.*

Exploiting the Paddlewheel Effect

Learn to take full advantage of the paddlewheel effect on your boat (Figure 2.28). It may be very different from boat to boat, depending on the weight, hull form and propeller type. Finding the best way to come alongside a quay is therefore a question of trial and error.

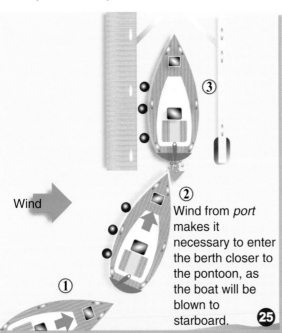

Wind

③
②
①

Wind from *port* makes it necessary to enter the berth closer to the pontoon, as the boat will be blown to starboard.

25

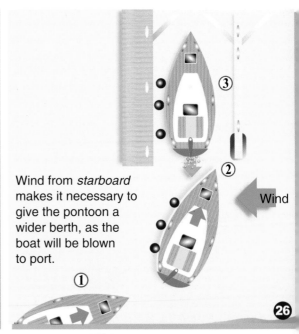

Wind from *starboard* makes it necessary to give the pontoon a wider berth, as the boat will be blown to port.

③
②
①

Wind

26

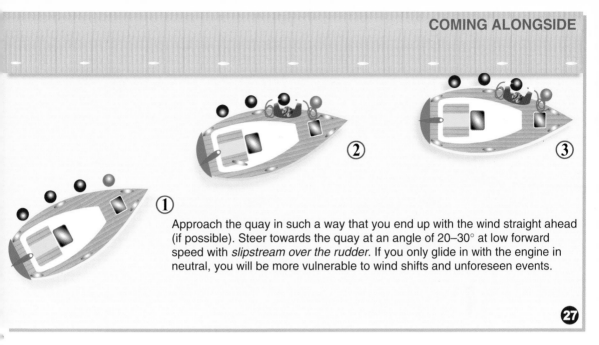

Approach the quay in such a way that you end up with the wind straight ahead (if possible). Steer towards the quay at an angle of 20–30° at low forward speed with *slipstream over the rudder*. If you only glide in with the engine in neutral, you will be more vulnerable to wind shifts and unforeseen events.

27

We will later describe methods that make you more independent of the paddlewheel effect when coming alongside, namely the use of spring lines. Then, you only need to make one single mooring line fast ashore in order to moor in a controlled manner by use of engine power. If you observe fishing boats, ferries and small freighters, you will see that they use spring lines all the time when coming alongside a quay.

EXPLOITING THE PADDLEWHEEL EFFECT

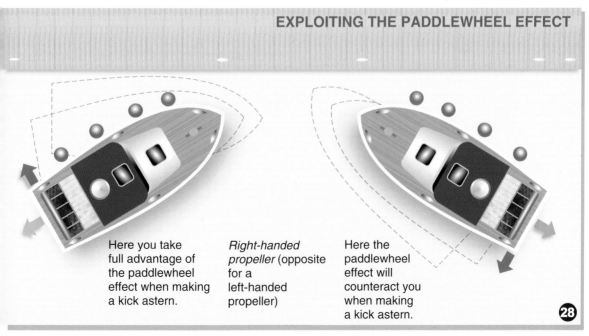

Here you take full advantage of the paddlewheel effect when making a kick astern.

Right-handed propeller (opposite for a left-handed propeller)

Here the paddlewheel effect will counteract you when making a kick astern.

28

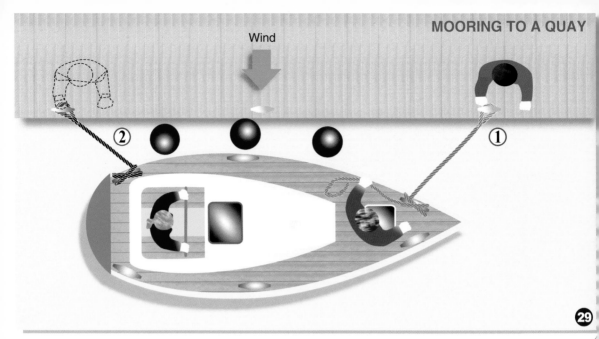

Wind

② ①

㉙

MOORING

Mooring to a Quay

When the boat is parallel to the quay, a crew member must be set ashore to take care of the mooring lines (or someone on the quay may be willing to assist you). If the wind is blowing out from the quay, the mooring must be done rather quickly (Figure 2.29). If not, the stern of the boat will be blown away from the quay before the crew has made fast a stern line (2). It is very difficult, and often downright impossible, to keep a yacht on to a quay with your hands with the wind off the quay, especially if the boat is of any size. Later, we will show how you can control your boat better with the use of a *spring line* and *engine power*.

When both *bow* and *stern lines* have been made fast, a *bow spring* and a *stern spring* have to be rigged. The function of the spring lines is to control the boat's movement *along* the quay; the *bow line* and *stern line* are used to prevent the boat drifting too far *off* the quay. This is standard mooring practice for pleasure yachts. If the boat doesn't have midships cleats, the springs will have to be fastened in the cleats fore and aft, as shown by the dashed lines in Figure 2.30. The *wind direction* decides the sequence of fastening the mooring lines.

If you want longer springs, they may be rigged as shown by the green, dashed lines. This is normally necessary where there are significant *tidal variations*.

Always use many fenders (you can never have enough and follow the old rule of *mooring for a storm*, as weather conditions may change radically in the course of minutes!

Mooring to a Quay using Spring Lines

When the boat has stopped close to the quay, a crew member must be set ashore to fasten a *bow spring* (Figure 2.31) (again, a person on the quay may assist). When the spring is made fast, the crew member shouts *'spring fastened!'* and the helmsman can now run the boat carefully in forward at the same time as the helm is put over(2). The bow spring prevents the boat from moving forwards and the *force on the rudder* pushes the stern inwards against the quay. *Don't stop the engine or put it in neutral yet! The key point about using a spring is that as soon as one single line has been made fast ashore, you are in complete control of your boat.*

When the boat is lying alongside the quay with *the engine running in forward* and *the rudder in the same position*, the helm can be locked and the helmsman can participate with the other mooring lines (Figure 2.32). *When all moor*

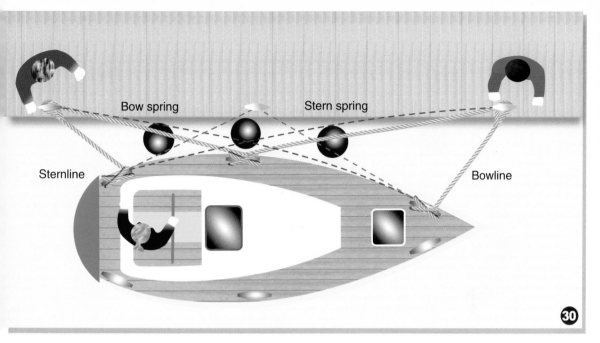

Bow spring   Stern spring

Sternline

Bowline

30

ng lines are made fast, you can stop the engine and lock he helm in neutral position. If you have problems getting he stern *close to the quay*, carefully increase the revs of he engine until you are satisfied. Note that hull shape and locations of fenders may make it impossible to get the stern against the quay. You don't have to do anything there and then if this is the case. But, little by little, you will find the optimum placement of fenders and the spring line under various conditions.

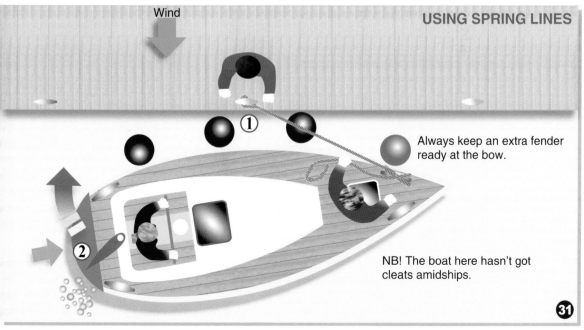

Wind

USING SPRING LINES

Always keep an extra fender ready at the bow.

NB! The boat here hasn't got cleats amidships.

31

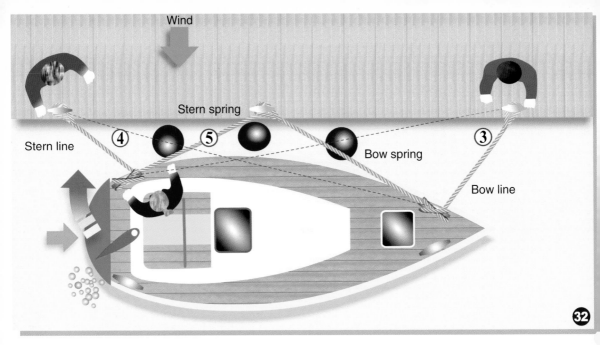

Wind

Stern spring

Stern line

④

⑤

Bow spring

③

Bow line

�932

USING BOW AND STERN SPRINGS

Entering a Narrow Berth using a Bow Spring

If there is just enough space between two moored boats, you may use a bow spring to 'squeeze' your boat in between them in a secure way (Figure 2.35). Approach the berth at a relatively big angle to the quay in order to avoid touching the other boats. When you are close enough to the quay, set a crew member ashore from the bow. When the bow spring is made fast, put the helm over and run the engine slowly in forward as usual. *Now the spring has to be adjusted under full control in order to get the boat securely into the berth.*

If necessary, the crew eases the spring in a controlled manner in order to get the bow close enough to the boat in front in such a way that the stern may pass the boat astern unobstructed. It is now important that the helmsman and the crew adjusting the spring communicate well. If everything is done calmly, it is possible to get a boat into a berth with only a small clearance to the boats in front and astern in this way (Figure 2.36). Remember though, never to moor a boat so close to others that they might be damaged if wind and sea pick up.

If you should change your mind after you have started the manoeuvre, or the space turns out to be too small, put the helm over to the opposite side. The stern will then move out again and if you let go of the spring when you are clear of both boats, you can slowly leave the berth going astern (See also Figures 2.37 and 2.38 for how to leave a berth on a bow spring).

Leaving the Quay using a Bow Spring

If you are about to leave when the wind is blowing *off the quay*, you can just let go all the mooring lines, leaving the sternline (Figure 2.37) until last. The bow will then blow away from the quay and you can sail away under sail or engine. If the wind blows *on to the quay*, however, it can be fairly difficult or downright impossible to get the bow out from the quay, especially when the boat is heavy. If you are without a *bow thruster*, a bow spring (1) may be used. First lead the bow spring back onboard. Start the engine and run it in *forward* with the helm as shown in Figure 2.37. Let go the bow line (2), stern spring (3) and finally the stern line (4).

The boat will still lie alongside the quay due to both the rudder force and the wind blowing against the quay. *Remember to put extra fenders at the bow!* When the crew is onboard and the bow spring has been rigged, the

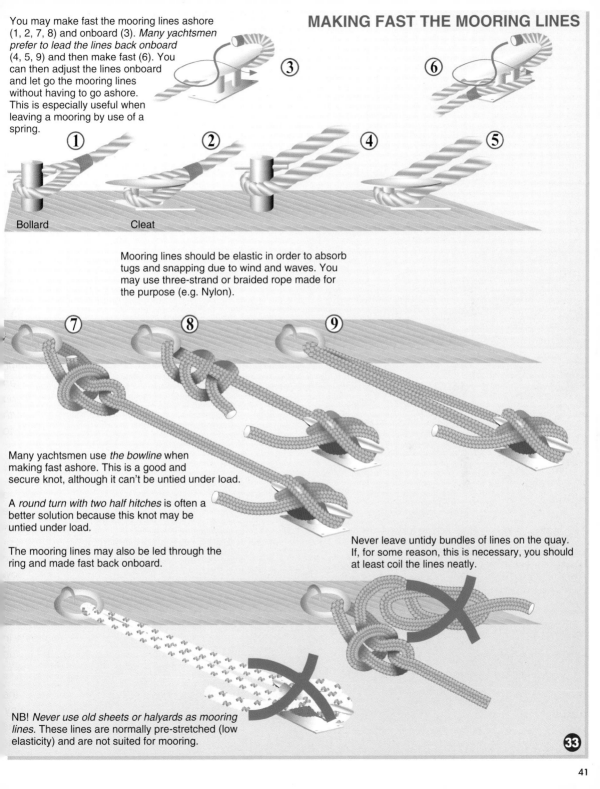

You may make fast the mooring lines ashore (1, 2, 7, 8) and onboard (3). *Many yachtsmen prefer to lead the lines back onboard (4, 5, 9) and then make fast (6).* You can then adjust the lines onboard and let go the mooring lines without having to go ashore. This is especially useful when leaving a mooring by use of a spring.

③

⑥

①

②

④

⑤

Bollard

Cleat

Mooring lines should be elastic in order to absorb tugs and snapping due to wind and waves. You may use three-strand or braided rope made for the purpose (e.g. Nylon).

⑦

⑧

⑨

Many yachtsmen use *the bowline* when making fast ashore. This is a good and secure knot, although it can't be untied under load.

A *round turn with two half hitches* is often a better solution because this knot may be untied under load.

The mooring lines may also be led through the ring and made fast back onboard.

Never leave untidy bundles of lines on the quay. If, for some reason, this is necessary, you should at least coil the lines neatly.

NB! *Never use old sheets or halyards as mooring lines.* These lines are normally pre-stretched (low elasticity) and are not suited for mooring.

33

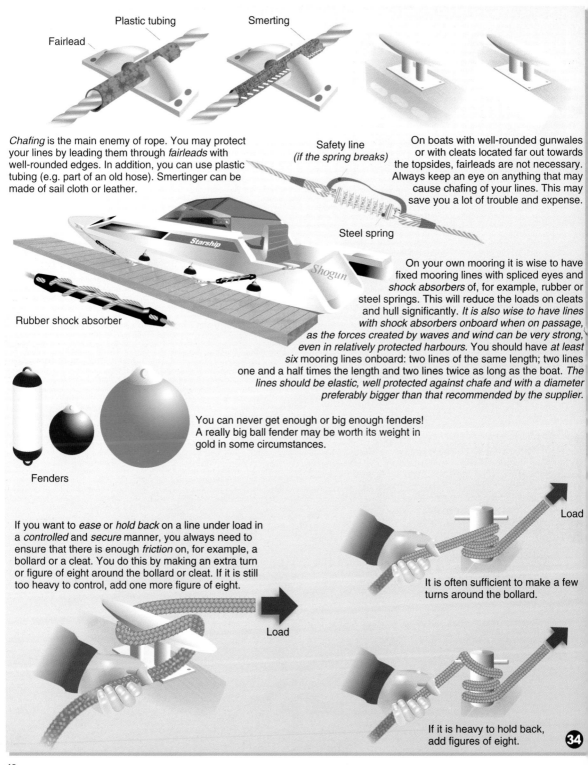

Fairlead — **Plastic tubing** — **Smerting**

Chafing is the main enemy of rope. You may protect your lines by leading them through *fairleads* with well-rounded edges. In addition, you can use plastic tubing (e.g. part of an old hose). Smertinger can be made of sail cloth or leather.

Safety line
(*if the spring breaks*)

Steel spring

On boats with well-rounded gunwales or with cleats located far out towards the topsides, fairleads are not necessary. Always keep an eye on anything that may cause chafing of your lines. This may save you a lot of trouble and expense.

Rubber shock absorber

On your own mooring it is wise to have fixed mooring lines with spliced eyes and *shock absorbers* of, for example, rubber or steel springs. This will reduce the loads on cleats and hull significantly. *It is also wise to have lines with shock absorbers onboard when on passage, as the forces created by waves and wind can be very strong, even in relatively protected harbours. You should have at least six mooring lines onboard: two lines of the same length; two lines one and a half times the length and two lines twice as long as the boat. The lines should be elastic, well protected against chafe and with a diameter preferably bigger than that recommended by the supplier.*

You can never get enough or big enough fenders! A really big ball fender may be worth its weight in gold in some circumstances.

Fenders

If you want to *ease* or *hold back* on a line under load in a *controlled* and *secure* manner, you always need to ensure that there is enough *friction* on, for example, a bollard or a cleat. You do this by making an extra turn or figure of eight around the bollard or cleat. If it is still too heavy to control, add one more figure of eight.

Load

Load

It is often sufficient to make a few turns around the bollard.

If it is heavy to hold back, add figures of eight.

34

42

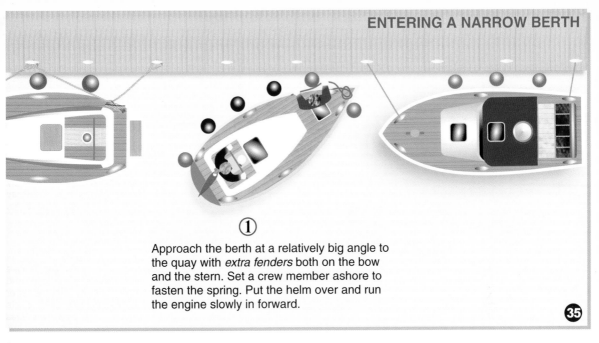

①

Approach the berth at a relatively big angle to the quay with *extra fenders* both on the bow and the stern. Set a crew member ashore to fasten the spring. Put the helm over and run the engine slowly in forward.

35

helm is put over. The stern will then be pushed out from the quay due to the slipstream over the rudder. When the stern is far enough out, the helmsman shouts, '*let the spring go,*' and puts the engine in neutral. The crew lets go the spring and pulls it quickly onboard, shouting, '*spring clear!*' The helmsman then puts the engine in reverse and goes astern out from the quay with the rudder in neutral (Figure 2.38).

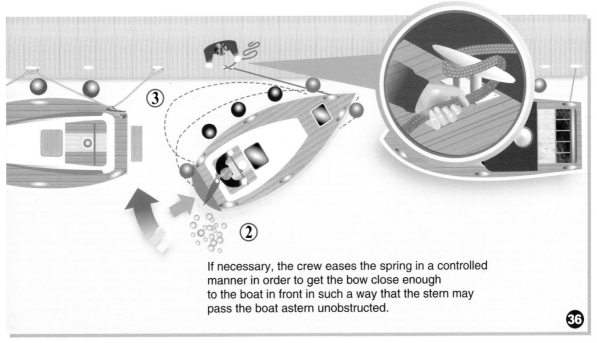

③

②

If necessary, the crew eases the spring in a controlled manner in order to get the bow close enough to the boat in front in such a way that the stern may pass the boat astern unobstructed.

36

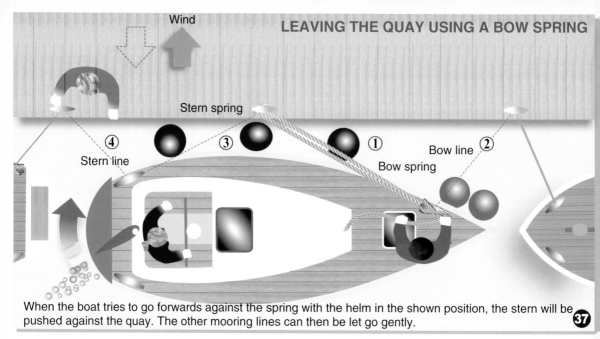

Wind

Stern spring

④ ③ ① Bow line ②

Stern line Bow spring

When the boat tries to go forwards against the spring with the helm in the shown position, the stern will be pushed against the quay. The other mooring lines can then be let go gently. **37**

With a bow spring it is possible to turn the bow at an angle of nearly 90° to the quay! The keys to success are preparation, communication, lots of fenders and calm execution. Try to practise all this in a quiet location.

Leaving the Quay using a Stern Spring

If the wind is not too strong you may leave the quay using a *stern spring* (Figure 2.39(1)). You can then move the bow out from the quay and sail away. You first lead

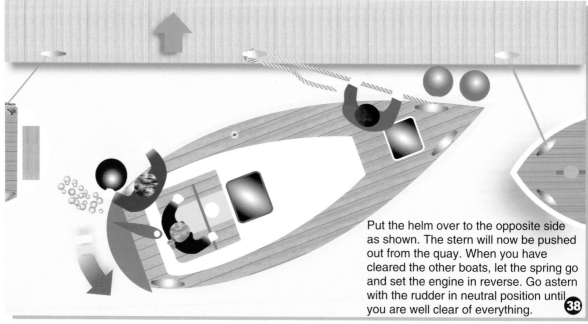

Put the helm over to the opposite side as shown. The stern will now be pushed out from the quay. When you have cleared the other boats, let the spring go and set the engine in reverse. Go astern with the rudder in neutral position until you are well clear of everything. **38**

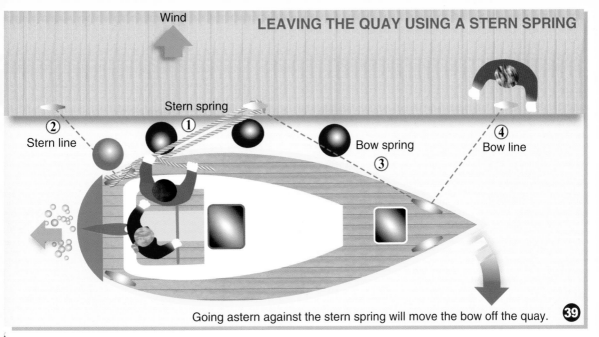

Wind

Stern spring

② ①

Stern line

Bow spring

③

④

Bow line

Going astern against the stern spring will move the bow off the quay. **39**

the stern spring back onboard. Start the engine and *run slowly in reverse* against the stern spring with the helm in neutral (rudder position has little effect now). Let go the stern line (2), bow spring (3) and then the bow line (4). When the crew is onboard, the helmsman increases the revs in reverse until the bow starts to move out from the quay. It may be necessary to hit full throttle before the bow moves. Remember an extra fender at the stern!

When the bow is well clear of the quay, the helmsman shouts, '*let go the spring,*' and puts the engine in neutral.

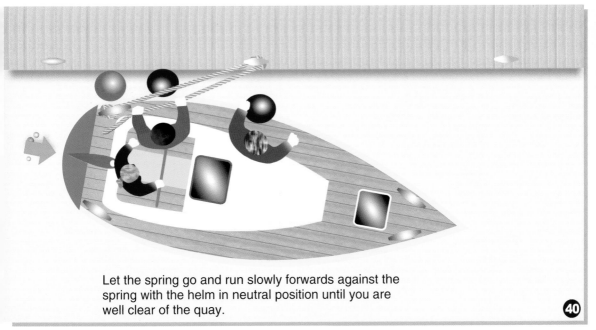

Let the spring go and run slowly forwards against the spring with the helm in neutral position until you are well clear of the quay. **40**

The crew unties the spring and pulls it quickly onboard (Figure 2.40). The helmsman sets the engine in forward and runs at slow speed out from the quay. *Keep the helm in neutral position until you are well clear of the quay – then you can put the helm over. Otherwise, the stern may 'skid' into the quay.*

Leaving a quay using a stern spring is not as effective as using a bow spring due to the reduced slipstream passing the rudder. Try out your own boat and see how much engine power is necessary to move the bow off the quay in various wind strengths. *When the wind is weak, it is normally very easy to leave a quay using a stern spring.*

'Springing' the Boat Around a Corner using a Stern Spring

When you want to go astern 'around a corner' and get the bow up into the wind or into a current, you may rig a *long stern spring* led back onboard. Let go the other mooring lines and start going astern out of the berth while the crew eases out on the spring. When the boat is well clear of the berth, the crew locks the spring (Figure 2.41). The boat will now turn into the wind (or the current). Continue going astern until the bow is close enough to the wind. Then go forwards and out while the crew quickly pulls in the spring (Figure 2.42).

Leaving the Quay Under Sail

With the wind blowing *on to the quay*, it is not possible to leave under sail if you don't row out an anchor, use help lines or a tug boat. When the wind blows *off the quay*, you may follow the procedure outlined in Figure 2.43. It is easiest to use only a foresail because the boom may cause problems if the wind is shifty – even if the main sail often gives better manoeuvrability.

Leaving the Quay in a Current

When there is a current, you may exploit this to leave the quay (Figure 2.44). You use the engine as usual, but you need less power because the current will help you. Leaving the quay under sail with a current is very complicated and is not recommended. If the wind blows *off the quay* it is possible, however, to sail with the current (against the current will be very difficult).

How Spring Lines Work

It is wise to practise using spring lines and get to grips with how they work. This may get you out of trouble and prevent damage to your boat. Even if your boat is equipped with a bow thruster, it is necessary to know how to use spring lines. (You can, for example, use a stern spring together with a bow thruster if the latter, for some reason, doesn't have enough power.)

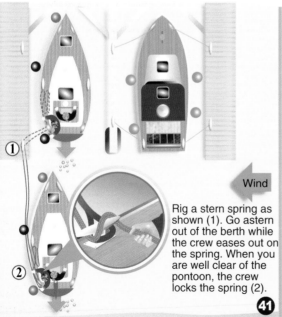

Rig a stern spring as shown (1). Go astern out of the berth while the crew eases out on the spring. When you are well clear of the pontoon, the crew locks the spring (2). **41**

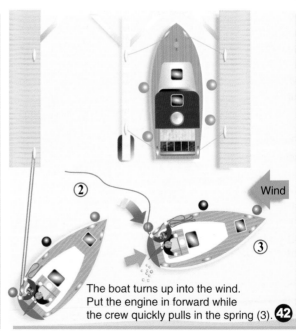

The boat turns up into the wind. Put the engine in forward while the crew quickly pulls in the spring (3). **42**

Let go both spring lines first.

Leaving by mainsail

Wind

☐ Hoist the main and take in on the sheet.
☐ Let go the bow line.
☐ When the bow begins to turn, let go the sternline and sail away from the quay.
☐ Set the foresail when you are well clear of the quay.

Leaving by foresail

Wind

☐ Set the foresail and take in on the sheet (back the foresail if necessary).
☐ Let go the bow line.
☐ When the bow begins to turn, let go the sternline and sail away from the quay.
☐ When there is enough room, luff and hoist the main.

43

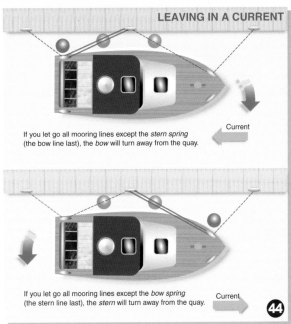

Current

If you let go all mooring lines except the *stern spring* (the bow line last), the *bow* will turn away from the quay.

If you let go all mooring lines except the *bow spring* (the stern line last), the *stern* will turn away from the quay. Current

44

How the Bow Spring Works

The bow spring (Figure 2.45) prevents the boat moving forwards as soon as the bow has made contact with the quay (normally via a fender). At the same time, the slipstream passing the rudder will create a sideways force that tries to turn the boat around the pivot point. This point will be where the spring line is fastened onboard and will not move when the bow is in contact with the quay and the spring line is taut. If you rig the spring from a midship cleat, it will be less efficient as the lever arm on which the rudder force will act, thus the turning momentum will be less.

How the Stern Spring Works

The stern spring (Figure 2.45) prevents the boat moving astern as soon as the stern has made contact with the quay (normally via a fender). The rudder force will, however, not work in the same way as for the bow spring, and the helm can therefore be kept in neutral position all the time. The engine power will try to pull the boat astern against the spring and the boat will start to turn around the pivot point where the spring has been made fast.

MORE ABOUT MOORING

It is always wise to make a small circuit first to have a look at the location before coming alongside a quay or mooring to buoys or piles. The skipper and helmsman must know the boat's handling characteristics well to be confident of completing these manoeuvres safely. Mooring lines, fenders and a boat hook should be made ready well in advance.

If you feel unsure as to whether you will be able to manoeuvre in a confined harbour with a lot of sidewinds, it is good seamanship to first moor where it is easier to do so, for example on the tip of the pontoon or alongside another boat. You may later haul your boat to the preferred berth or you may require help from other yachtsmen in the harbour.

Yachts are normally moored *bow to wind* in order to be more sheltered in the cockpit and the companionway.

It is important that the mooring lines are not totally taut. The boat will then be subject to a lot of tugs and jerks. Ease the mooring lines a bit so the boat is free to move a little without danger of hitting other boats or obstacles (Figure 2.46). Mooring lines equipped with shock absorbers may be tightened more.

Winding Ship

Warping a boat around end-to-end in her berth is called *winding ship*. You use lines led fore and aft, as shown in Figure 2.47(a). If you want to warp the boat around in order to have the bow to the wind, use the lines shown in Figure 2.47(b).

Boats Moored in a Raft

In crowded harbours, boats are often moored alongside each other in so-called *rafts*, with bow and stern lines and springs between them. *If it is possible, it is important to lead lines ashore from each boat. This may be difficult, but at the very least, every third boat should have bow- and sternlines ashore. Sailing yachts should be moored bow to stern to prevent the rigs hitting each other. Always ask permission to moor alongside another boat, even if it is a tradition that should be accepted readily. Remember to have enough fenders ready!*

If you are moored between two boats and want to leave the raft (Figure 2.47(c)), you should leave *with the wind* (or current if it is dominating). Otherwise the outermost boats may drift away uncontrolled. If your boat is the out-ermost one, you just leave in the same way as you would leave a quay. *You should always make an agreement with the other boats before leaving. Sometimes it is necessary to set a crew member from your own boat onboard a neighbouring boat to pull the raft back in afterwards.*

Mediterranean Moor

Mooring with the stern to the quay and a bow anchor is used a lot in the Mediterranean. This is often called a *Mediterranean moor* (Figure 2.48(a). It may be difficult going astern into a vacant berth and dropping the anchor at the same time, especially in strong sidewinds.

Leaving the Quay when Moored to Piles

When leaving the quay, you take the fenders in on deck. You then use the *slip lines* at the bow or stern (or both) to guide the boat out between the piles (Figure 2.49(b)).

Mooring to Piles Under Sail

When approaching a pile under sail, you must study both the wind and current carefully (Figure 2.52). If the current is the stronger, it may be best to sail *against the current*. If the wind is strongest, it will often be safer to sail *into the wind*.

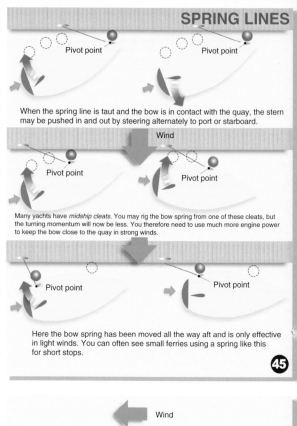

SPRING LINES

When the spring line is taut and the bow is in contact with the quay, the stern may be pushed in and out by steering alternately to port or starboard.

Wind

Many yachts have *midship cleats*. You may rig the bow spring from one of these cleats, but the turning momentum will now be less. You therefore need to use much more engine power to keep the bow close to the quay in strong winds.

Here the bow spring has been moved all the way aft and is only effective in light winds. You can often see small ferries using a spring like this for short stops.

45

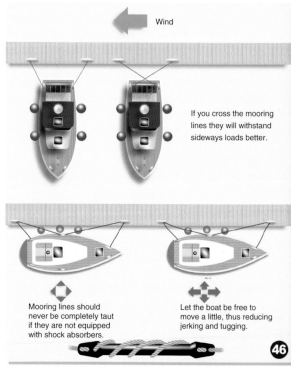

Wind

If you cross the mooring lines they will withstand sideways loads better.

Mooring lines should never be completely taut if they are not equipped with shock absorbers.

Let the boat be free to move a little, thus reducing jerking and tugging.

46

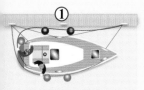
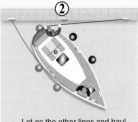
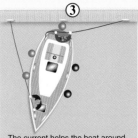
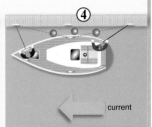

① Lead the new bow line (red) around and outside the pulpit, guard rail and rig and then ashore. The new stern line (blue) should be led around and outside the pushpit, guard rail and rig and then ashore.

② Let go the other lines and haul on the blue stern line to initiate the turn. Take in all slack when hauling the red bow line.

③ The current helps the boat around. Take in all slack. Use a boat hook to push the stern out.

④ Pull the boat in to the quay and rig bow and stern spring lines.

current

(a)

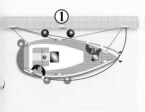
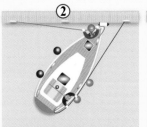
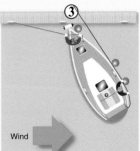

① Rig new bow and stern lines.

② Let go the other mooring lines and haul the boat around (the wind will help).

③ Wind

④ Pull the boat in to the quay and rig bow and stern spring lines.
Be careful when warping the boat around in strong winds or currents, especially if your is big and heavy.

(b)

BOATS MOORED IN A RAFT

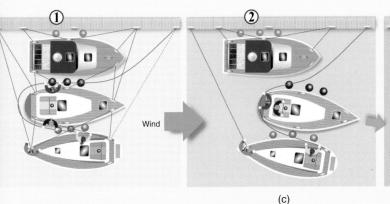

① Wind

②

③ *Note that when going ashore from a boat moored outside another, you should always cross the foredeck if possible.*

(c)

Leaving the raft.

Lead the outermost boat's stern line (*red*) around the stern of your boat and make it fast ashore. (If you want to leave the raft going astern, you will have to lead the outermost boat's bow line forward of the bow of your own boat and ashore).

Let go all mooring lines of the outer and inner boat and leave the raft. The crew of the outside boat pulls it (or uses a winch or engine) alongside the inner boat, taking in the slack on the stern line.

The outer boat has been pulled alongside the inner one and all mooring lines have been made fast.

 47

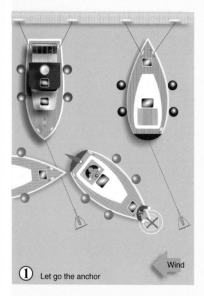

① Let go the anchor

Wind

Drop the bow anchor, leaving sufficient distance from the quay. In sidewinds you have to let go the anchor farther to windward. (the problem is that, more often than not, you don't know the whereabouts of the anchors of other boats).

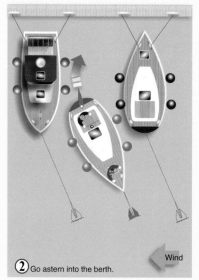

② Go astern into the berth.

Wind

(a)

Start going astern as soon as the anchor hits the bottom and keep a *good steering speed* while paying out on the anchor line. If the bow is blown to leeward, you can try to hold back a little on the anchor line to get the bow more into the wind.

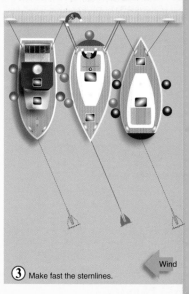

③ Make fast the sternlines.

Wind

When you are 1–2 m from the quay, set the engine in forward to stop the boat and fasten the anchor line. A crew member is set ashore to make fast the sternlines (first to windward). *Use a lot of fenders! Don't take any chances doing acrobatics when jumping ashore.*

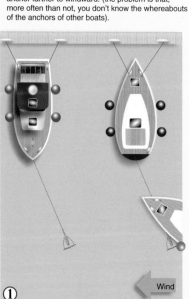

①

Wind

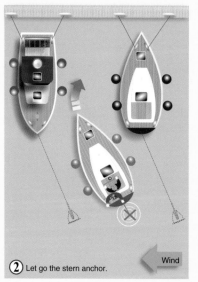

② Let go the stern anchor.

Wind

(b)

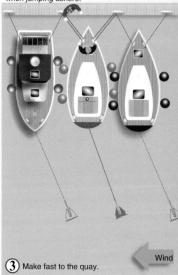

③ Make fast to the quay.

Wind

Mooring Bow to Quay with a Stern Anchor in Strong Sidewinds

In strong sidewinds, a simpler solution may be to drop a *stern anchor* and go forwards, mooring the bow to the quay as shown for the blue boat.

Drop the anchor. Go forwards into the berth with adequate steering speed while paying out the anchor line. Back up 1–2 m from the quay and at the same time fasten the anchor line. A crew member is then set ashore to fasten the bow (windward line first). *Take in on the anchor line so the boat remains a safe distance from the quay.*

48

Morring Bow to Quay and Stern to Piles

In some marinas you have to moor the stern to piles and the bow to the quay or vice versa (Figure 2.49(a)). The piles may be equipped with permanent mooring lines, but normally you have to use your own lines.

You may also back the boat in between the piles and moor the *stern* to the quay. But this is more complicated. You then rig slip lines from the bow and *lead them aft* in order to gain more time to put them around the piles.

You need to maintain relatively good steering speed astern to go between the piles. In sidewinds you go closer to the windward pile and reduce speed just when the crew is going to put the lines around the piles.

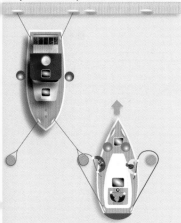

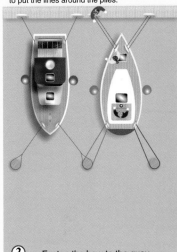

①   Put the slip lines around the piles.

Make slip lines ready on both sides and lead them forwards (to the shrouds on a sailboat) to gain more time to pass them around the piles. In sidewinds, you go closer to the windward pile.
Keep good steering speed all the time and have fenders ready.

②   Pay out on the slip lines.

Don't place the fenders before you have passed the piles. They may set the boat totally off course if they are squeezed between the hull and the piles. The crew pays out on the slip lines while trying to straighten the boat by holding back a little on one of the sides.

③   Fasten the bow to the quay.

When close enough to the quay, the crew is setashore to fasten the bow lines (first to windward). Then you fasten and adjust the stern lines. *With only two people onboard, the helmsman has to handle one of the stern lines.*

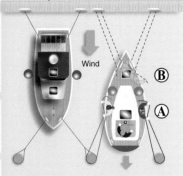

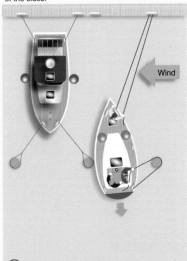

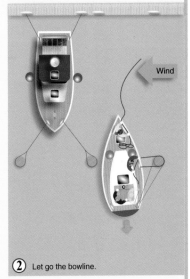

Method A:
Move the two aft slip lines amidships. Let go the bow lines and pull the boat astern using the slip lines. When the bow is between the piles, you let go of them and back out.

Method B (dashed lines):
Rig extra long slip lines forward. Let go the sternlines and pay out on the slip lines, passing between the piles. Then let go the slip lines and back out.

With the wind *straight from behind*, you let go in the bow and back slowly out while using the aft slip lines as extra guides. *Headwinds* are more difficult because the bows may blow away from the wind. Use slip lines to guide the boat and keep the course straight.

① Let go the leeward mooring lines and back out.   **②** Let go the bowline.

In sidewinds, you first let go the leeward mooring lines. Back out while paying out on the bow line and taking in on the stern line. The boat will drift down to leeward and you guide it between the piles by adjusting the bow and stern lines. When the piles are near amidships, you may have to move the stern line (dashed) forwards in order to be able to *pull the boat clear of the leeward pile.* When clear, you let go the bow line and back out while guiding the boat with the slip line, which you finally let go.

Mooring to Piles

Wind and Current have the Same Direction

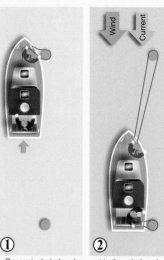

Leaving

① Go *against* wind and current to the *windward pile*. Pass a slip line around it (1) and let the boat *drift down to the leeward pile* while paying out on the bow line. Pass a slip line around the pile (2).

② ③ Pull (or run) the boat to windward while paying out on the stern line and take in on the bow line until the boat is located centrally between the piles. Make fast the lines (3).

④ Leaving the mooring...

⑤ Pay out on the bow line (4) and let go the stern line. When you are close to the leeward pile (5), go *forwards* to one of the sides while letting go the bow line (6).

⑥ It is also possible to just let go both mooring lines and go out from position 3 with the rudder to either side (but this is a bit less secure).

Keep the line clear of the propeller!

Leaving

Leaving the mooring...

Wind and Current are in Opposite Direction (current strongest in this example)

① You may here use the method described above. It is the safest if the wind blows along the piles. But you may also go against the current to the first pile (1) and pass the stern line around it. Then go to the other pile

② ③ while paying out on the sternline. Pass the bow line around this pile (2) and let the boat drift back while adjusting the mooring lines (3). When between the piles, make fast the lines.

④ Leaving the mooring...

⑤ You may leave as shown above or you may do the following: Let go the stern line and then the bow line (4) while running the engine in forward with *just enough revs to stem the current* (and the wind), keeping the boat still relative to the piles. Put the helm slightly to starboard (5) and the boat

⑥ will slide sideways to starboard. When it is clear of the piles (6), increase the revs and go forwards and away. *With sidewinds you may use the techniques described below when mooring and leaving.*

50

Current and Sidewinds

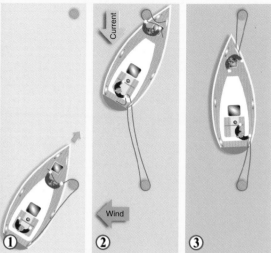

Leaving

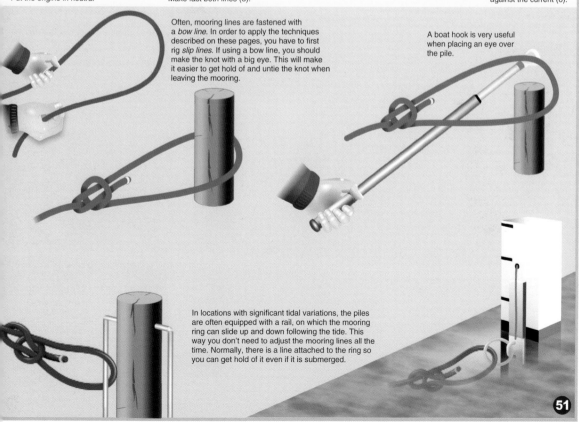

① ② ③ ④ ⑤ ⑥

Go *at an angle to the wind up* to the first pile. Pass a slip line around it (1) and go slowly in the same direction, letting the wind blow the boat on to the next pile. Put the engine in neutral

and pass a slip line around the pile (2). Pay out on this line and take in on the stern line until the boat is central between the piles. Make fast both lines (3).

Leaving the mooring...

When leaving, pay out on both mooring lines, letting the boat blow to leeward of the piles (4).

When you are clear of the piles, let go both mooring lines (5) and then go away against the current (6).

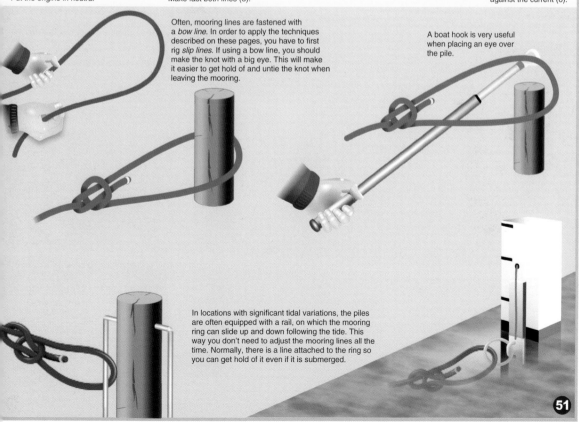

Often, mooring lines are fastened with a *bow line*. In order to apply the techniques described on these pages, you have to first rig *slip lines*. If using a bow line, you should make the knot with a big eye. This will make it easier to get hold of and untie the knot when leaving the mooring.

A boat hook is very useful when placing an eye over the pile.

In locations with significant tidal variations, the piles are often equipped with a rail, on which the mooring ring can slide up and down following the tide. This way you don't need to adjust the mooring lines all the time. Normally, there is a line attached to the ring so you can get hold of it even if it is submerged.

51

Wind Forward of the Beam and Current

Wind | Current

Leaving

Wind | Current

① ② ③ | ④ ⑤ ⑥

Sail on a *close reach* between the piles and *luff into the wind* so the boat will have lost all speed when the windward pile is almost amidships (2). Quickly pass a slip line around the pile. Take down the sail and let the boat drift down to the leeward pile, passing a stern line around it. Pull the boat in between the piles and make fast (3), as shown in previous examples.

Leaving the mooring...

To leave the mooring, just hoist the *main sail*, tighten the sheet and steer away from the piles while paying out on the bow line (4). The *current passing the rudder* makes the boat easier to turn. First let go the stern line (5) and then the bow line.

When you are well clear of the piles you can hoist the foresail (6). (If the boat won't turn, you may *hoist and back the jib* earlier to force the bow to bear away to either side at 4.)

Wind on the Quarter and Current

Current

Wind

Leaving

Current

Wind

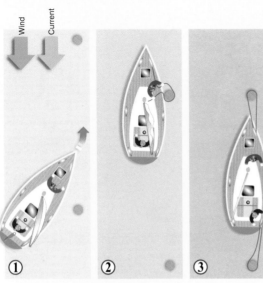

① ② ③

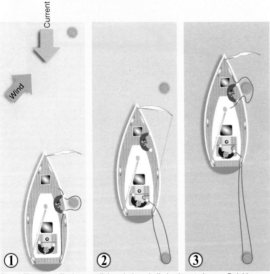

④ ⑤ ⑥

Reach/Run on a *jib* alone until the windward pile is almost abeam. Quickly pass a stern line around the pile and continue to the next pile while paying out on the stern line (2). Pass a bow line around this pile (3). The boat speed can be controlled with the jib sheet and the stern line can be used as a brake until the bow line is secured. Then let go the jib sheet and take down (or roll in) the sail. Let the boat drift with the current (or pull it) towards the first pile while paying out on the bow line and taking in on the stern line, until the boat is positioned between the piles. Then make fast the mooring lines.

Leaving the mooring...

To leave the mooring, just hoist the jib, tighten the sheet and steer away from the piles while paying out on the bow line (4). The *current passing the rudder* makes the boat easier to turn.

Let go both mooring lines (5) and reach/run away from the piles. When you are well clear of the piles, *luff* and hoist the *main sail*.

52

54

Lead the mooring line through the mooring ring on the buoy and back onboard. You can then leave quickly and securely under all conditions.

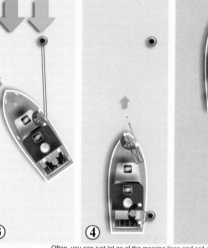

① ② ③ ④

Go against *the current* (or wind if it is the stronger) up to the buoy and reduce the speed evenly until the boat has stopped just at the buoy. Don't back too hard, as you may then push the buoy away from the boat.

Lead the bow line through the mooring ring on the buoy and back onboard and let the boat drift back a little while paying out on the bow line (2). Then make fast. (You may, of course, make fast directly to the ring.)

Leaving the mooring...

Often, you can just let go of the mooring lines and sail away from a buoy. If you want to leave on a specific course, you can re-rig the slip line as shown (3). If you want to moor between *two buoys* to prevent the boat from turning in wind or current, rig a slip line at the first buoy (4). Then go to the next buoy, make fast the bow (5) and let the boat drift back a little.

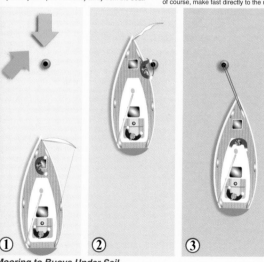

① ② ③ ④ ⑤ ⑥

Mooring to Buoys Under Sail
Wind and Current are in Opposite Directions
(current strongest in this example)

Reach/run against the current up to the buoy with only a jib set. Adjust the speed with the sheet to have the boat stopped when the buoy is just forward of the beam (2). Lead the bow line through the mooring ring on the buoy and back onboard. Let the boat drift back a little, paying out on the bow line and make fast (3).

Leaving the mooring...

Put the helm over, set the jib, let go the bow line and steer away from the buoy (4). With wind from an unfavourable direction (5), just rig a new slip line and let go the first one.

Set the jib when the bow has borne away and let go the slip line (6). By using slip lines you may leave a buoy quite easily in any direction.

Some buoys are equipped with mooring lines. Check them thoroughly and preferably use them in addition to your own mooring lines.

A lesser buoy is attached to some buoys; you can pick this up with a boat hook.

53

Mooring to Buoys

Wind and Current have the Same Direction

In some places you have to moor either the bow or the stern to buoys or you have to moor to buoys both fore and aft. In these situations you can use almost the same techniques as when mooring to piles. *Always check that the buoys are big enough for the size of your boat*.

Mooring to buoys both fore and aft is much used in *estuaries* and *canals* in order to prevent the boat turning in wind or current. Such mooring makes it necessary to have a dinghy onboard if you wish to go ashore.

TIDES

When tidal variations are significant, it is always easiest to moor at *high tide*. You should use *very long mooring lines* in order to compensate for the varying water level. The *bow* and *stern lines* must be fastened far from the boat so that the angles will be acceptable even when the water is ebbing. This way you don't have to adjust these lines all the time. But in order to prevent the boat from drifting too far from the jetty, weights (e.g. an anchor) could be put on these lines, as shown in Figure 2.54. If the crew is onboard, the spring lines should be adjusted from time to time. If everybody leaves the boat, you have to be absolutely sure that the spring, bow and stern lines *are long enough at low water*.

'SPRINGING' THE BOAT AROUND A CORNER II

Figures 2.41 and 2.42 showed how you could turn around a corner using a stern spring. You may also use a *bow spring* to achieve the same result. Rig a long bow spring as a *slip line* (Figure 2.56). Let go the other mooring lines (the stern spring last) and leave the berth along the pontoon (the wind blows you away from it). When clear of the pontoon, lock the spring (2) and the boat will turn into the wind (or current). Let go and take in the spring quickly (3). *This technique may also be used to turn around piles.*

MORE ABOUT SLIP LINES

It is very important that slip lines can run easily around or through the fixation point ashore, in such a way that you can free the line quickly and retrieve it onboard. *When leaving a berth using a spring or another slip line, you must anticipate what will happen if the slip line should get jammed ashore*. If you have ensured that it can run freely you will have no problems. If you *absolutely can't take* the chance that the spring gets stuck, you may use the method shown in Figure 2.57 (1–2). Make figures of eight around the cleat with both ends of the line at the same time. When you let go the spring, first try to take it in in the normal way. If it turns out to be jammed, throw both ends ashore (the line may be picked up later). Alternatively, you may cut the line, but that normally takes too long.

Check water depth at *low tide* and find out where ladders are located on the quay.

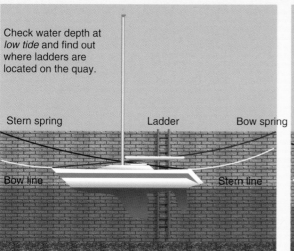

Stern spring | Ladder | Bow spring

Bow line | Stern line

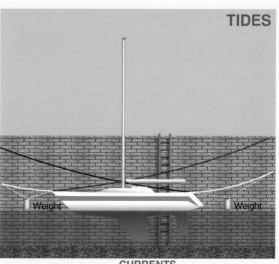

Weight | Weight

CURRENTS

When the current is significant you should always try to go *against* it, both under sail and power. When you are coming alongside a quay or pontoon in particular, it is very easy to misjudge the speed of the boat if you are going with the current. In contrast, you will have an extra 'brake' if you are coming alongside against the current. To get a feel for the current's direction and speed, you can look at spars and buoys and also other boats and dinghies moored to buoys or swinging to an anchor. *It is important that the crew has been briefed on how you plan to come alongside.*

Try to steer *straight against the current* with just enough power for the boat to make *no speed over ground*. You can then see that the boat doesn't move relative to spars, buoys or objects ashore. Now, if you put the helm over a little, the boat will go *sideways* through the water. This is a technique (*ferry-gliding*) which is very useful when coming alongside or leaving a quay in strong currents. *Wind and currents may be more complicated than shown in the examples in this book. If you have any doubts it may be wise to wait some time for the conditions to improve.*

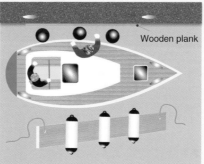

Wooden plank

When you moor to a quay or pontoon with an uneven surface, e.g. an old brick quay, it is wise to use a wooden plank against the wall of the quay in order to protect the boat and the fenders. This is also wise in some old locks. The *tidal range* may vary from zero to more than 15 metres, depending on where in the world you are located.

It is very important to know how the boat will behave if it is *to dry out at the bottom* at low tide. This is especially important for fin-keeled sailing yachts. *If in doubt, don't hesitate to ask other sailors for advice. Never leave the boat unattended for long periods in places with great tidal ranges without being totally confident of your mooring!*

It is important to prevent the boat from *toppling over outwards* when it hits the bottom at low tide. You can secure the boat with a line from the quay to a *tight halyard* onboard using a pulley (1) or a shackle (2) that can slide along the halyard when the water level changes.

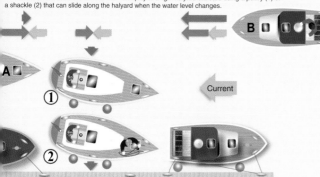

A | B | Current | (1) | (2)

Currents have a great impact on a boat. Imagine that the boat behaves as described earlier but *at the same time* is moved by the *speed* and *direction* of the current.

Boat A makes 3 knots through the water (normally the speed shown on the log). But the current runs with a speed of 2 knots in *the opposite* direction. Therefore, the boat makes only 1 *knot over ground* (3 − 2 = 1).

Boat B also makes 3 knots through the water but is going *with* the current. It therefore makes 5 *knots over ground* (3 + 2 = 5).

If boat A reduces speed to 2 knots through the water and the course is altered by 5–10° (1), it will move *slowly sideways over ground* into the berth (2).

 Speed over ground  Speed through the water

 54

Manoeuvring in Currents

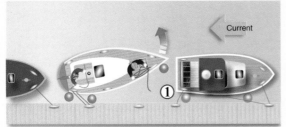

In a *counter current* it is safest to leave the pontoon using a *stern spring*. Let the current turn the bow (or back a little) away from the pontoon. Then quickly put the engine in forward with sufficient revs so that the spring goes slack

and then let it go. Put the helm over and the current will swiftly move the boat sideways away from the pontoon. Increase the revs and leave going against the current.

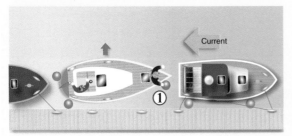

A more daring method is to first put the engine in forward with just enough revs to neutralize the current (the stern spring goes slack). Let go all mooring lines and put the helm over a little so the boat glides sideways out from the pontoon (2).

You are very vulnerable when all mooring lines have been released. Therefore, the helmsman needs to handle the engine and helm cautiously. *Have many fenders and mooring lines ready in case problems occur.*

Bow Thrusters

A tube made from GRP or metal is mounted through the hull, forming a *tunnel* in which a propeller can push the water to either side, creating a sideways force on the boat.

Bow thrusters are normally driven by electric motors via an *angular drive*.

Some bow thrusters can be lowered down from the hull when in use. This avoids the tunnel, which creates friction when sailing. However, this type of thruster is more vulnerable than the ones with a tunnel.

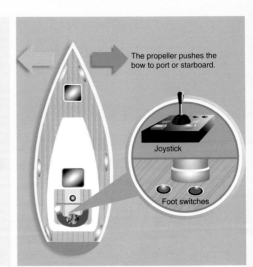

The propeller pushes the bow to port or starboard.

Joystick

Foot switches

Many yachts are equipped with a bow thruster, which makes manoeuvring in confined spaces easier. However, if this applies to your boat, you should still learn the techniques described in this book. *Sooner or later the thruster may fail due to flat batteries or, for example, a plastic bag stuck in the tunnel.*

Bow thrusters are often very noisy. Therefore, it is wise to limit their use on arrival and departure to avoid disturbing other people unnecessarily. Using a spring should be the standard procedure. The bow thruster should be used in difficult situations or when you feel unsure.

The bow thruster is normally operated by two *foot switches* on deck or by a *joystick* at the helm position, i.e. the pedestal in sailing yachts. You may also combine use of the bow thruster with a stern spring if, for any reason, there is a lack of power.

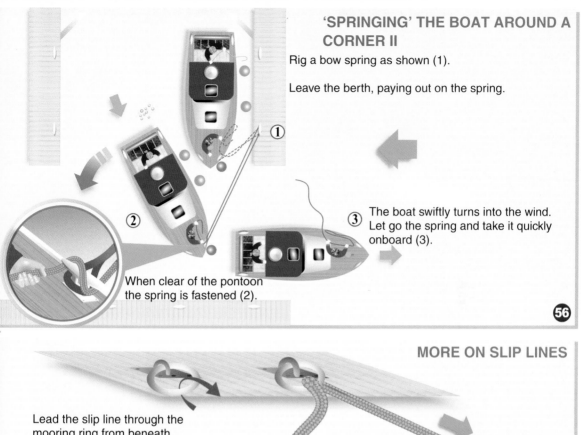

'SPRINGING' THE BOAT AROUND A CORNER II

Rig a bow spring as shown (1).

Leave the berth, paying out on the spring.

③ The boat swiftly turns into the wind. Let go the spring and take it quickly onboard (3).

When clear of the pontoon the spring is fastened (2).

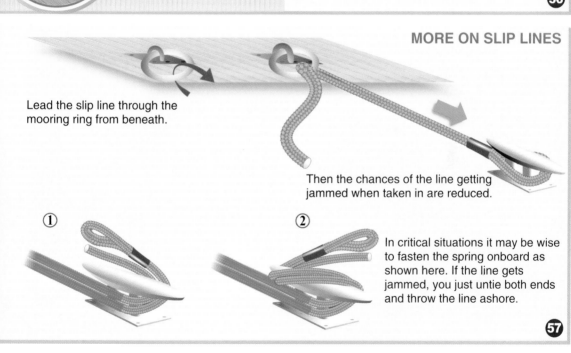

MORE ON SLIP LINES

Lead the slip line through the mooring ring from beneath.

Then the chances of the line getting jammed when taken in are reduced.

In critical situations it may be wise to fasten the spring onboard as shown here. If the line gets jammed, you just untie both ends and throw the line ashore.

Anchoring

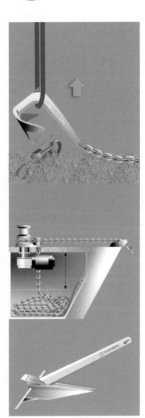

M|any yachtsmen prefer to anchor in a distant, peaceful bay away from the overcrowded, noisy and, not least, expensive marinas. In order to anchor safely it is necessary to know some basic techniques that will stand you in good stead until experience makes you a more competent and knowledgeable sailor.

Always remember that the ground tackle (anchor, anchor rode, shackles, etc.) is a vital part of the safety equipment onboard. Therefore, everybody going out to sea should have a thorough understanding of what the required ground tackle is and how this equipment should be handled.

THE BASICS

When anchoring, it is the anchor's ability to *dig itself into the seabed* that holds the boat in place – not the weight alone. Therefore, the seabed should be composed of *sand, gravel, clay*, etc. so that the anchor has the best chance of digging itself in. Rocks, stones and sea grass make a poor seabed for anchoring.

The pull on the anchor should always be *along the bottom* in order for the anchor to dig in and down into the seabed. This is achieved by letting out so much chain and rope that, however strong the pull becomes, the chain is never lifted completely from the seabed.

This means that you normally have to let out a length of the rode 4–7 times the *water depth*.

It is also necessary to have a minimum of 5 metres of chain behind the anchor. The rest of the *anchor rode* (line, chain or a combination of both) may be line (rope). The chain part is necessary to avoid strong *chafing* and *breakage* of the rode near the anchor due to sharp rocks, coral, etc. It makes life much easier to use an anchor rode comprised of chain only, even if this means increasing the weight forward.

You let go the anchor at the chosen spot when all forward movement has stopped. You then let the wind blow you astern (or back the boat cautiously) until enough rode has been laid out along the seabed (Figure 3.1(1)). The anchor rode can now be made fast and you then ensure that the anchor will dig into the seabed properly by *backing slowly* at first (Figure 3.1(2)), then increasing the revs to almost maximum (Figure 3.1(3)) while observing if the boat stops moving astern relative to *objects ashore*.

If the boat still moves astern, first try letting out 5–6 metres of extra rode. Then try backing again. If the anchor won't hold, you must retrieve the anchor and try again.

It is important that these principles are followed when you are either *swinging to a bow anchor* or, for example, the bow is moored to a quay or a rock with a stern anchor holding the bow out from land.

If the boat is swinging to a bow anchor, it is important that there is enough *swinging room* to allow for the wind shifting during the night (Figure 3.2). You should always be aware of other boats and any possibility that your boat could move into too shallow water.

Using *two anchors* may be necessary in order to compensate for big shifts in wind or current. Typically, you may anchor in a fresh sea breeze during the daytime, which dies out in the evening. The land breeze at night may be quite strong and in the opposite direction. If you have only anchored with a bow anchor, it may easily be pulled loose and start to *drag along the seabed*. The relative impacts of wind and current on the boat may also change significantly due to, for example, a change of tide.

Sometimes it may be necessary to use two anchors *in tandem* (one anchor behind the other) to avoid dragging

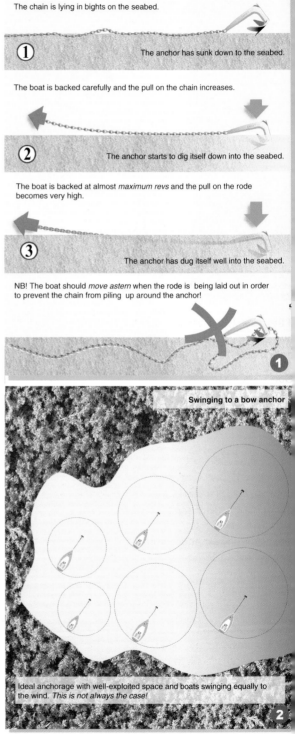

The chain is lying in bights on the seabed.

① The anchor has sunk down to the seabed.

The boat is backed carefully and the pull on the chain increases.

② The anchor starts to dig itself down into the seabed.

The boat is backed at almost *maximum revs* and the pull on the rode becomes very high.

③ The anchor has dug itself well into the seabed.

NB! The boat should *move astern* when the rode is being laid out in order to prevent the chain from piling up around the anchor!

1

Swinging to a bow anchor

Ideal anchorage with well-exploited space and boats swinging equally to the wind. *This is not always the case!*

2

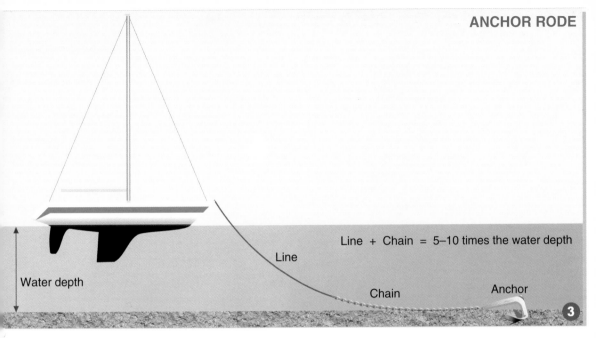

Line + Chain = 5–10 times the water depth

Line

Water depth

Chain

Anchor

3

f the wind speed should increase too much. (The use of two anchors will be described in more detail later in the chapter.)

Good seamanship when anchoring is, as with other aspects at sea, the ability to estimate possible changes of weather, wind and currents, and then prepare to compensate for these changes in due time.

THE ANCHOR RODE

Traditionally, it was common for pleasure boats to use a combination of a short length of *chain* and a *long line* for the anchor rode (Figure 3.3). Nowadays, many yachtsmen use only chain. In any case, you should have at least have five metres of chain next to the anchor, as mentioned earlier, as there is always a danger of sharp rocks or corals on the seabed cutting a rope line. In some countries it is mandatory to carry a length of chain at least three times the overall length of the boat.

Braided rope with a *lead core*, and thus some of the chain's advantages, does exist, although this type of rode may be difficult to handle.

t is very important that the pull on the anchor is as horizontal as possible (Figure 3.4). This is best achieved with chain only. If, for any reason, you choose to use a combination of chain and line, you should use an *anchor chum* (weight), as shown in Figure 3.24, in order to obtain a more horizontal pull on the anchor.

There are also anchor lines made from flat bands of *Nylon webbing* stored on reels, which can be mounted on the pulpit, pushpit, stanchions, etc. The webbing band is very light and strong, although it can be a bit difficult to handle under load. Some metres of chain will also be necessary with this type of anchor rode to guard against chafing on the seabed. The band runs easily from the reel and can be reeled in with a winch handle. This type of webbing band is used mostly for *stern anchors* and *kedges*, as the band is light and a bit tricky to belay on, for example, a cleat.

GROUND TACKLE

Anchors

Pleasure boats should be equipped with *at least two anchors*. Smaller, lighter boats can use a *kedge* as the second anchor. Long-distance cruising boats are often equipped with three anchors. Some of the commonest types of anchor used to be the *Bruce* and *CQR* anchors, in addition to a heavy *Fisherman* for really hard weather (Figure 3.5).

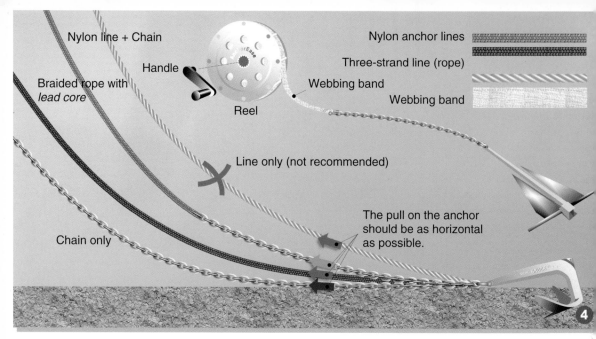

Nylon line + Chain

Handle

Braided rope with *lead core*

Reel

Webbing band

Nylon anchor lines

Three-strand line (rope)

Webbing band

Line only (not recommended)

Chain only

The pull on the anchor should be as horizontal as possible.

4

The *Bruce anchor*, which was made for drilling rigs, has been one of the most popular anchors on yachts. This anchor digs in well in sand, gravel and mud, but is less reliable on rocks and bottoms with lots of seaweed. The Bruce anchor is easy to handle, as it has no movable parts, although it can sometimes be difficult to break loose when weighing anchor. It stows well on a bow roller but is a bit bulky in anchor wells.

The *CQR anchor* is also very popular in long-distance cruisers. It is forged in galvanised steel and the hinged shank makes the anchor handle wind shift well. It digs in well in sand, gravel, mud and seaweed-covered bottoms, although it may take some time before it holds well. It is easy to break loose when weighing anchor. However, it may be a bit difficult to handle and stow.

As the patents on the Bruce and CQR anchors have expired, there are a lot of cheap copies of the originals on the market. These are mostly made of galvanized cast iron and are of varying quality.

The *Danforth anchor* is well suited for sand and mud but less suited for rocky bottoms or bottoms covered by seaweed. The anchor is somewhat difficult to handle, although it is easy to stow.

The *Delta anchor* has some of the same properties a the CQR but is difficult to handle. It stows well only on bow roller.

The *Rocna anchor* from New Zealand and the Sarca anchor from Australia are two more recent ancho designs with an alleged ability to dig in quickly due t their special design with a *semicircular hoop* around th crown (Figure 3.6).

Modern, lightweight anchors made from aluminium, lik the *Fortress anchor*, have impressive holding power i relation to weight (Figure 3.6). Made of special alloys they have almost the same strength as steel but only ha the weight. They are easy to handle and stow, althoug difficult to break loose while weighing anchor.

The Fortress anchor is very much used as the mai anchor in the USA, where there are a lot of sandy an muddy seabeds. It is not so well suited for rock, cora and seaweed-covered seabeds.

There is no perfect anchor for all seabed and weathe conditions. Different opinions about the various ancho types exist. It may, however, be worth considering a ligh weight anchor like the Fortress in addition to the trad tional Fisherman, Bruce and CQR anchors.

For dinghies, small, folding anchors or Bruce anchors are commonly used.

Anchor Sizes

When you have chosen the type of anchor you want to use, you have to decide the necessary size. This depends mainly on the boat's *length* and *displacement*. Only thorough experience gained from repeated real-life visits to actual areas under different prevailing weather conditions will indicate the ideal size of your chosen anchor. *Never accept the supplier's recommendations at face value. Check out, for example on the Internet, what experienced long-distance cruisers can tell you about the properties of a specific type of anchor.*

Be aware that tests in yachting magazines may be very misleading because they often only expose the anchor to a steadily increasing load until it breaks out of the seabed. The pull is almost horizontal, as these tests frequently are made in shallow water on a beach. *In reality, an anchor is exposed to strongly varying loads, both in strength and direction. A constant horizontal pull would require an almost infinitely long anchor rode at the depths you normally would drop your anchor.*

If you are planning a long passage you need a *storm anchor.* This will necessarily be quite heavy. For many anchor types you should double the weight recommended by the suppliers (Figure 3.7). If you only need an anchor for day trips under relatively good weather conditions, you may use lighter anchors. It is always wise, however, to spend money on a big, heavy anchor. Of course, you have to ensure that it can be handled, even in bad weather, either manually or by a windlass.

Chain

Anchor chain is normally made of *galvanised steel*. It is also available in *stainless steel*, although the latter is much more expensive. The advantage of a stainless steel chain, in addition to reduced corrosion, is that its smooth surface is easier to keep clean.

Mark the chain with *colour codes* every five metres along its length, so you always know how much chain you have laid out. Both mechanical and electronic counters exist, although it is wise to mark the chain all the same.

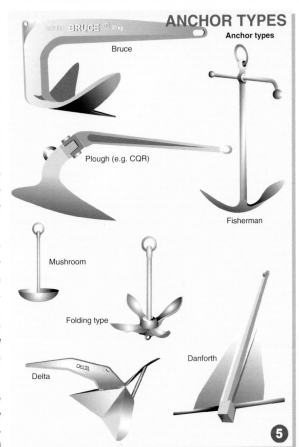

ANCHOR TYPES

Anchor types

Bruce

Plough (e.g. CQR)

Fisherman

Mushroom

Folding type

Danforth

Delta

5

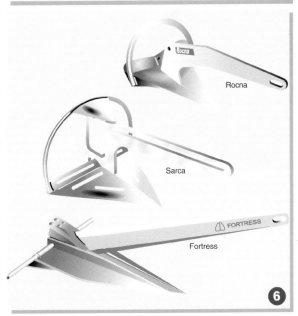

Rocna

Sarca

Fortress

6

A swivel (Figure 3.8) between the chain and anchor prevents the rode getting entangled. It may save you a lot of frustration.

Anchor Shackles

Shackles come in various types. D-shackles with *unbraco type bolts* (Figure 3.8) are good for joining chain lengths. The bowed part of the shackle should point towards the anchor in order to avoid jamming when the rode is running out quickly.

Bow Rollers

Long-distance cruisers more often than not use double bow rollers (Figure 3.8). Many anchors can be stowed in the bow roller but either have to be lashed or secured with a bolt on longer passages.

Many yachts also have a roller on the stern, which is especially useful in Scandinavian waters when mooring the bow to a rock or quay.

Chain Hooks

Chain hooks (Figure 3.8) are used to lock the anchor or to relieve the windlass, as shown later in Figure 3.23.

Anchor Windlasses

It is sometimes heavy work weighing (taking up) the anchor, and on a slippery deck in a seaway it may even be dangerous. A windlass will give you added strength and may save your back!

Windlasses used to be big, heavy and expensive. Nowadays, they have become so reliable, compact and cheap that they are installed on even smaller yachts.

There are several different types of windlass, including:

• *Manual windlasses*, which are operated by a winch handle. These are cheaper and easier to install than electrical and hydraulic windlasses, and require no electrical supply.

• *Electrical windlasses*, which are connected to the boat's electrical circuits and are operated by deck-mounted foot switches, panel switches or by remote control. Most electrical windlasses can be operated manually in case of loss of electrical supply.

• *Hydraulic windlasses*, which are used mostly on bigger yachts with additional hydraulic gear, for example

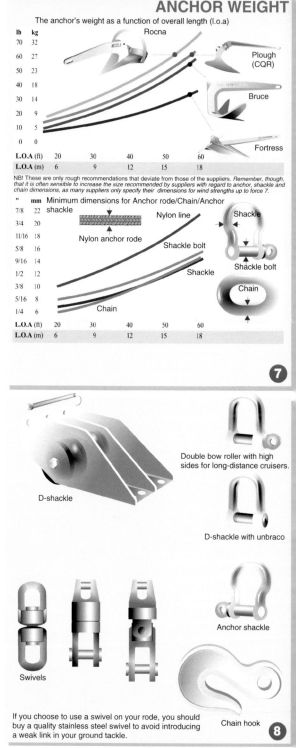

ANCHOR WEIGHT

The anchor's weight as a function of overall length (l.o.a)

lb	kg					
70	32				Rocna	
60	27					Plough (CQR)
50	23					
40	18					Bruce
30	14					
20	9					
10	5					
0	0					Fortress

L.O.A (ft)	20	30	40	50	60
L.O.A (m)	6	9	12	15	18

NB! These are only rough recommendations that deviate from those of the suppliers. *Remember, though, that it is often sensible to increase the size recommended by suppliers with regard to anchor, shackle and chain dimensions, as many suppliers only specify their dimensions for wind strengths up to force 7.*

"	mm	Minimum dimensions for Anchor rode/Chain/Anchor
7/8	22	shackle
3/4	20	
11/16	18	
5/8	16	
9/16	14	
1/2	12	
3/8	10	
5/16	8	
1/4	6	

Nylon line
Nylon anchor rode
Shackle
Shackle bolt
Shackle
Shackle bolt
Chain
Chain

L.O.A (ft)	20	30	40	50	60
L.O.A (m)	6	9	12	15	18

7

D-shackle

Double bow roller with high sides for long-distance cruisers.

D-shackle with unbraco

Swivels

Anchor shackle

If you choose to use a swivel on your rode, you should buy a quality stainless steel swivel to avoid introducing a weak link in your ground tackle.

Chain hook

8

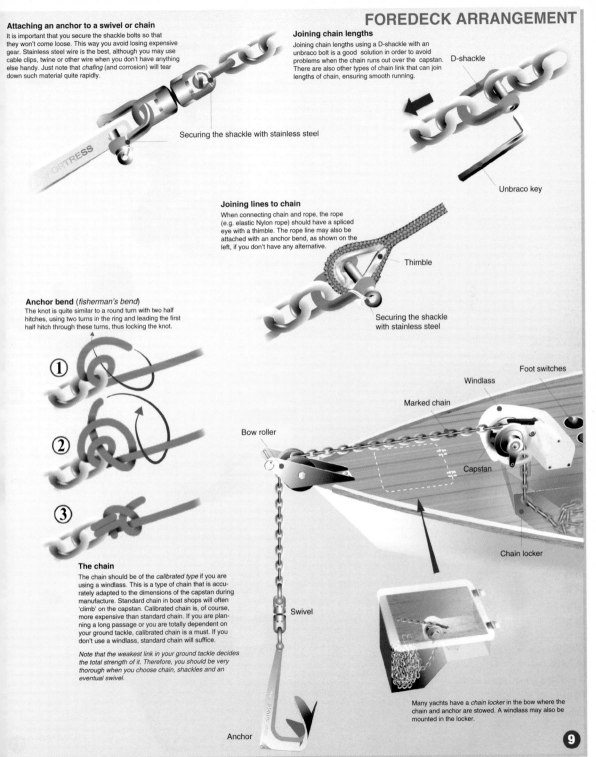

Attaching an anchor to a swivel or chain

It is important that you secure the shackle bolts so that they won't come loose. This way you avoid losing expensive gear. Stainless steel wire is the best, although you may use cable clips, twine or other wire when you don't have anything else handy. Just note that *chafing* (and corrosion) will tear down such material quite rapidly.

Securing the shackle with stainless steel

Joining chain lengths

Joining chain lengths using a D-shackle with an unbraco bolt is a good solution in order to avoid problems when the chain runs out over the capstan. There are also other types of chain link that can join lengths of chain, ensuring smooth running.

D-shackle

Unbraco key

Joining lines to chain

When connecting chain and rope, the rope (e.g. elastic Nylon rope) should have a spliced eye with a thimble. The rope line may also be attached with an anchor bend, as shown on the left, if you don't have any alternative.

Thimble

Securing the shackle with stainless steel

Anchor bend (*fisherman's bend*)

The knot is quite similar to a round turn with two half hitches, using two turns in the ring and leading the first half hitch through these turns, thus locking the knot.

① ② ③

The chain

The chain should be of the *calibrated type* if you are using a windlass. This is a type of chain that is accurately adapted to the dimensions of the capstan during manufacture. Standard chain in boat shops will often 'climb' on the capstan. Calibrated chain is, of course, more expensive than standard chain. If you are planning a long passage or you are totally dependent on your ground tackle, calibrated chain is a must. If you don't use a windlass, standard chain will suffice.

Note that the weakest link in your ground tackle decides the total strength of it. Therefore, you should be very thorough when you choose chain, shackles and an eventual swivel.

Foot switches

Windlass

Marked chain

Bow roller

Capstan

Chain locker

Swivel

Anchor

Many yachts have a *chain locker* in the bow where the chain and anchor are stowed. A windlass may also be mounted in the locker.

⑨

bow thrusters. Otherwise, installing a hydraulic windlass may be very expensive.

Windlasses are either of a *horizontal* or a *vertical* type (Figure 3.10). The latter will have a motor mounted below deck (better corrosion protection) and can be very compact. Even though the horizontal type is easy to install, the vertical type has many advantages: a larger part of the chain is in contact with the chain gypsy and the chain may be led onto the gypsy at various angles to the centreline.

It is advantageous for the windlass to have both a *chain gypsy* and a *rope drum* or a *combined chain and rope gypsy*, which is common on modern low-profile windlasses. This way, your windlass can be used for other purposes onboard.

On boats without an anchor windlass, a *chain stopper* (pawl) mounted on the bow roller or between the bow roller and the windlass may be of great help when weighing anchor (Figure 3.11). When taking in on the chain, the pawl will just flip upwards as each link passes. When you want to take a rest, you just let go of the chain. The pawl will prevent the chain from running out. If you want to pay out more chain, just flip the pawl backwards.

Chain Lockers

Chain lockers should be deep, providing sufficient free fall of the chain to maintain its self-stowing capacity (Figure 3.11). Otherwise, the chain will have a tendency to pile up in a cone until it tips over and the chain may become jammed. You will only notice this the next time the anchor is set! Therefore, it is often better to have the chain locker located closer to the centre of the boat. It may then be made deeper and, in addition, the weight of the chain will be closer to the boat's centre of gravity. Chain lockers should be equipped with a drain in order to prevent corrosion of the chain.

Always join the end of the chain with a rope long enough to have the end of the chain pulled out on the foredeck in a critical situation, either to join a new length of chain or to cut the rode and let everything go overboard. Fasten the rope inside the chain locker.

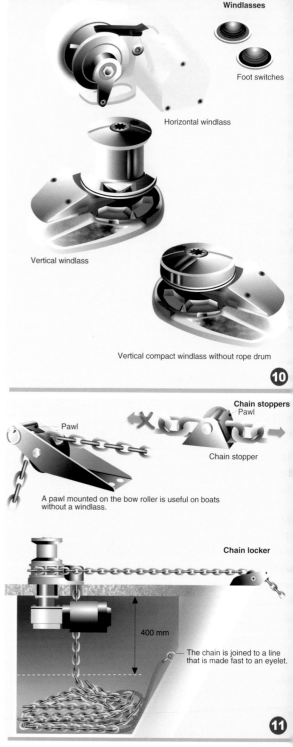

Windlasses

Foot switches

Horizontal windlass

Vertical windlass

Vertical compact windlass without rope drum

(10)

Chain stoppers
Pawl

Pawl

Chain stopper

A pawl mounted on the bow roller is useful on boats without a windlass.

Chain locker

400 mm

The chain is joined to a line that is made fast to an eyelet.

(11)

ANCHORING TECHNIQUES

What Makes a Good Anchorage?

The most important thing is that the anchorage is well protected against waves and wind and has a good holding ground. Good anchorages are marked on sea charts for pleasure vessels with an anchor symbol.

Theoretically, the ideal water depth when anchoring should leave you with a minimum clearance of 50 cm at low tide. *But bear in mind that the seabed is not absolutely flat and waves may be generated, making it necessary to ensure an extra clearance to be safe.*

Preparations for Anchoring

Before you drop the anchor you should make thorough preparations, especially when there are other yachts around. Make the anchor ready to go and check that the anchor rode may run out freely. Lay out about ten metres on deck, as shown in Figure 3.12. Be careful to ensure that the chain will not run out accidentally if the boat makes a sudden heel. *Always be careful not to stand in the middle of the chain when you let it run out. You should have great respect for anchor chain, as it might be dangerous if used carelessly!*

If you have got a windlass you should check that the brake/clutch works properly before dropping the anchor.

Remove all sails from the foredeck and take in lines being dragged through the water. If you are using the engine, the main sail should be stowed properly in advance.

Anchoring

Go by engine or sail straight into the wind or current (whichever is the dominant) towards the point where you want to drop the anchor. When the boat has stopped completely, drop the anchor and let the rode run out until the anchor hits the seabed. Then drift (if you don't have an engine) or power astern slowly as the crew pays out on the rode in a controlled manner, ensuring that it is laid out in an approximately straight line along the seabed. When enough rode has been laid out, set the engine in neutral and make the rode fast on a cleat or attach the brake. Look at objects ashore (trees, navigation marks, etc.), preferably abeam, and note how the boat comes

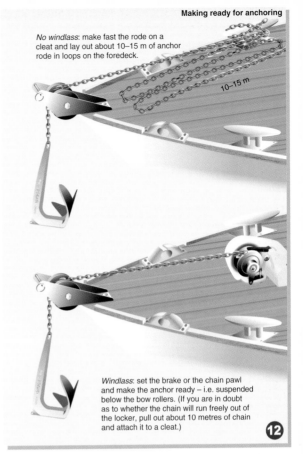

Making ready for anchoring

No windlass: make fast the rode on a cleat and lay out about 10–15 m of anchor rode in loops on the foredeck.

10–15 m

Windlass: set the brake or the chain pawl and make the anchor ready – i.e. suspended below the bow rollers. (If you are in doubt as to whether the chain will run freely out of the locker, pull out about 10 metres of chain and attach it to a cleat.) **12**

Recommended scope (Ratio between the length of the rode and the water depth)

Anchoring conditions	Chain	50% Rope + 50% chain	Rope + a little chain
Short stops – Fair weather	3	4	4
Overnight – Fair weather	4	5	6
Moderate weather	6*	7	8
Hard weather	7*	8	10

* chain with relieving line (see Figure 3.23)

Catenary (from Latin catena = chain) is a measure of the anchor rode's curvature due to its weight.

Water depth

Length of the rode

If you, for example, have laid out 20 m of anchor rode and the water depth is 4 m, you get: *Scope* = 20/4 = 5 **13**

to a halt. The anchor rode will lift itself out of the water as the anchor begins to hold. *Now the helmsman should set the engine in slow astern again, watching the objects ashore until the bearings no longer change* (the rode sinks and then lifts itself again as loops on the seabed are straightened out). *When you are sure that the boat no longer moves astern, slowly increase the revs to nearly full astern. If the bearings on the objects ashore don't change and the crew members no longer feel any jerking or vibrations when they grip the rode, the engine should be set in neutral and then stopped.*

The boat will now be pulled forwards due to the weight of the rode and will finally find its position of equilibrium. Make a final check of the bearings ashore and hoist the anchor ball sign (daytime) or a white anchor light (night signal) forward.

Note the difference in necessary scope between chain only and combinations of chain and rope shown in Figure 3.13. The swinging room will be significantly reduced when using chain only. In addition, the boat will 'wander' around less because it then has to drag a loop of chain over the seabed. The weight of a chain-only rode, however, may be a problem for smaller, lighter boats, and chain is significantly more expensive than rope, although the anchoring techniques are more or less the same whatever type of anchor rode you use.

Anchor signals are mandatory, making it easier for other boats to see that you are swinging to an anchor (Figure 3.14). Note that at night it is easier to detect a lower hanging anchor light than the type that is often found above the tricoloured navigation light at the top of the mast on sailing yachts. *It is not easy to have to stare 15–20 metres up in the air when you are trying to find an anchorage at night among many other anchored boats.*

Anchor Buoys

Anchor buoys are very useful in order to indicate the position of an anchor – either your own or the anchors of other boats (Figure 3.14). The use of anchor buoys has become rarer these days, although in many places, for example the Mediterranean, the seabed is littered with old chains and wrecks. In such places, an anchor buoy attached to the *anchor crown* would be a smart move in case the anchor should get stuck on any rubbish.

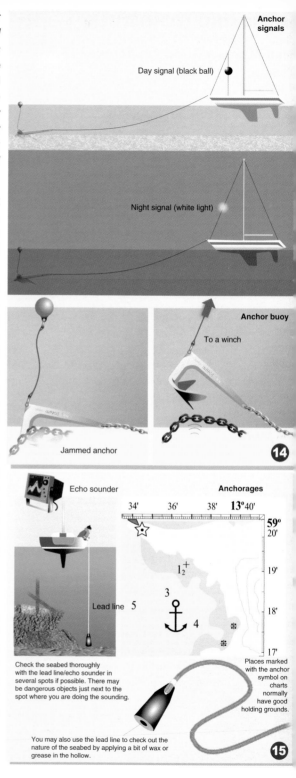

Anchor signals

Day signal (black ball)

Night signal (white light)

Anchor buoy

To a winch

Jammed anchor

(14)

Echo sounder

Lead line 5

Anchorages

34'   36'   38'   **13°40'**

59°
20'

19'

18'

17'

Check the seabed thoroughly with the lead line/echo sounder in several spots if possible. There may be dangerous objects just next to the spot where you are doing the sounding.

Places marked with the anchor symbol on charts normally have good holding grounds.

You may also use the lead line to check out the nature of the seabed by applying a bit of wax or grease in the hollow.

(15)

he problem with anchor buoys is that other people ften think they may use them as mooring buoys! Or ney mistake them for crab pots that may be emptied. Of course it is possible to mark the buoy with the name f the boat, although this isn't easily seen in the dark. ong-distance cruisers, therefore, often use empty plas-c bottles as anchor buoys.

Finding a Good Anchorage

When looking for a good anchorage, first have a look on ne chart for marked anchorages that will protect against ny expected wind, waves and currents (Figure 3.15). If ne *tidal range* is of a significant magnitude, you should heck the depth of both *high* and *low tides* (see also igure 3.22).

When anchoring in new places you should take a little ime to make soundings, either with an echo sounder r a lead line, in order to ensure a relatively even bot-om without big rocks, wrecks, etc. A lead line with a ead weight on the end often has a small hollow on the inderside of the weight. With a little wax or grease in the ollow, you may retrieve small samples of the seabed Figure 3.15). Here are some codes used on charts for arious types of seabeds:

- **S** = sand
- **M** = mud

- **Cy** = clay
- **G** = gravel
- **St** = stones
- **R** = rock.

Always check the depth with the lead line or echo sounder to confirm your calculations when there is a tidal range of some magnitude. Also note that the tabulated heights are only approximate and that the real depth may devi- ate from the tables.

Try to get a good picture of the swinging circles of the other boats in the anchorage. Boats with mainly rope rodes will have a tendency to 'sail around' the anchor more than boats with all-chain rodes. Boats with much windage and/or shallow depths are more likely to 'wan- der' around in the anchorage.

Anchoring using One Anchor

When anchoring with only one anchor (Figure 3.16), you go straight against the wind and stop the boat com- pletely when the desired drop point has been reached. The anchor is then dropped, paying out quickly on the rode until the anchor hits the bottom. Now start going slowly astern, paying out the rode in a controlled

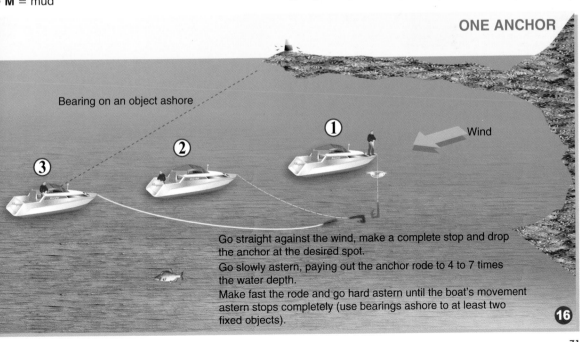

ONE ANCHOR

Bearing on an object ashore

① Wind

②

③

Go straight against the wind, make a complete stop and drop the anchor at the desired spot.
Go slowly astern, paying out the anchor rode to 4 to 7 times the water depth.
Make fast the rode and go hard astern until the boat's movement astern stops completely (use bearings ashore to at least two fixed objects).

16

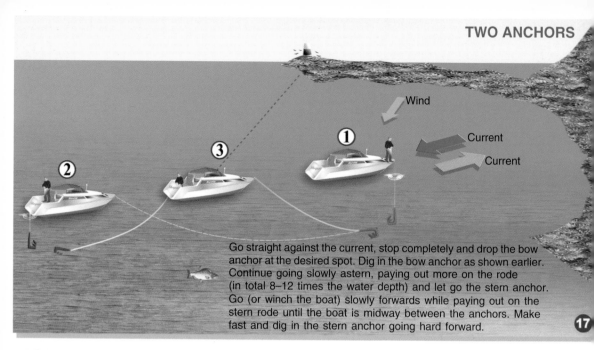

Go straight against the current, stop completely and drop the bow anchor at the desired spot. Dig in the bow anchor as shown earlier. Continue going slowly astern, paying out more on the rode (in total 8–12 times the water depth) and let go the stern anchor. Go (or winch the boat) slowly forwards while paying out on the stern rode until the boat is midway between the anchors. Make fast and dig in the stern anchor going hard forward.

17

manner. When enough rode has been laid out, back up hard on the engine until the bearings ashore stop changing, showing that the boat doesn't move astern anymore. *This is the basic anchoring technique, which you use when no great changes in wind or current direction are expected when lying at anchor.*

Anchoring using Two Anchors

When anchoring for longer periods, when big changes in wind and current direction are likely, you should use *two anchors*. When, for example, the *tide* is dominating, you go against the current and drop the *bow anchor* at the desired spot (Figure 3.17(1)) and back up, digging the anchor in as explained earlier. When the anchor holds, go slowly astern, paying out on the rode until you reach the position where you want to drop the *stern anchor* (2) and let it go. Go slowly (or pull using a winch) forwards while paying out on the stern rode and taking in on the bow rode until you are in a position midway between the anchors (3). Make fast the stern anchor and dig it in by going hard forward. (Using two anchors will be described in more detail later).

Anchoring Under Sail using One Anchor

Sailing yachts with auxiliary engines can use the techniques shown above. If you want to (or have to) anchor

without the use of an engine (Figure 3.18), you ma sail up to the drop point and *luff* straight into the wind dropping the anchor when the boat has lost all its forward speed. The problem is that the bow will bear awa quickly. The weight of the chain will help keep the bow into the wind and you may try pulling lightly on the rode from time to time and then continue paying out. *With thi technique the anchor will not dig in properly before being exposed to sufficient load from wind and waves.*

Digging in the Anchor Under Sail

In order to get the anchor to dig in deeper, you may use the technique illustrated in Figure 3.19. Reach or run towards the drop point with only a foresail set. Let go the anchor when you pass the drop point (1) and quickly pa out on the rode in a controlled manner. When enough rode has been paid out, make fast the rode (2). The boat will now spin into the wind and the anchor will dig in (3) Adjust the boat's speed during this operation either by rolling in the jib or letting go the sheet from time to time You may also back the sail to increase the speed astern after the boat has stopped. *If you have enough swinging room it is quite easy to anchor under sail, especially your rode is mostly chain, although you will never be sur that the anchor has dug in properly, unlike when using an engine.*

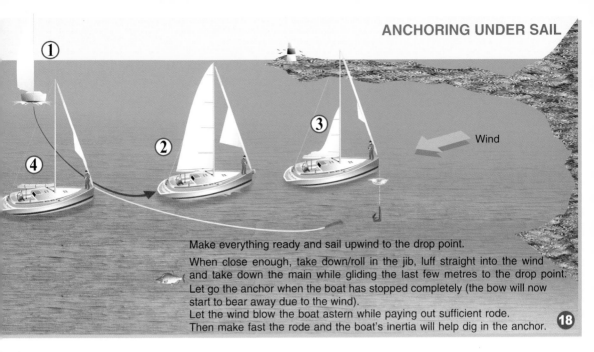

Make everything ready and sail upwind to the drop point.

When close enough, take down/roll in the jib, luff straight into the wind and take down the main while gliding the last few metres to the drop point. Let go the anchor when the boat has stopped completely (the bow will now start to bear away due to the wind).
Let the wind blow the boat astern while paying out sufficient rode.
Then make fast the rode and the boat's inertia will help dig in the anchor.

18

Anchoring Under Sail using Two Anchors

If you want to anchor using *two anchors* in the example from Figure 3.18, let the boat drift much further astern and then drop the second anchor (Figure 3.20(2)), which may be a stern anchor or another bow anchor with the rode led from the bow. (You can also shackle this second rode to your main bow anchor rode.) Then pull/winch the boat forwards with the bow rode while

DIGGING IN THE ANCHOR UNDER SAIL

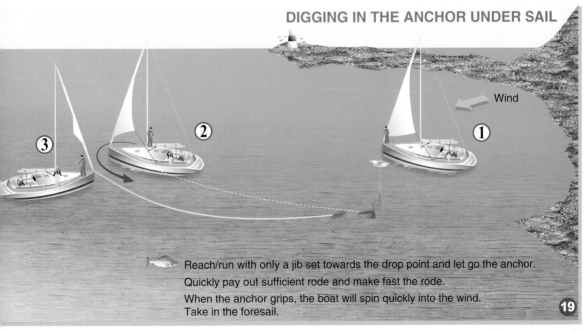

Reach/run with only a jib set towards the drop point and let go the anchor.

Quickly pay out sufficient rode and make fast the rode.

When the anchor grips, the boat will spin quickly into the wind.
Take in the foresail.

19

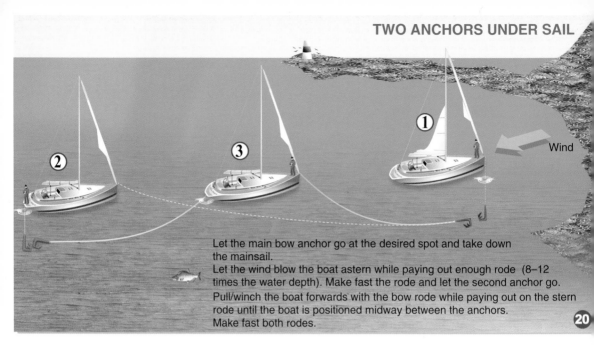

Let the main bow anchor go at the desired spot and take down the mainsail.

Let the wind blow the boat astern while paying out enough rode (8–12 times the water depth). Make fast the rode and let the second anchor go.

Pull/winch the boat forwards with the bow rode while paying out on the stern rode until the boat is positioned midway between the anchors. Make fast both rodes.

20

letting out on the stern rode until the boat is positioned midway between the anchors (3). Make fast the rodes. *This method is not without its weaknesses: it is difficult to have the boat drift astern in a controlled manner and the anchors will not dig in properly.*

Digging in the Bow Anchor and Dropping Stern Anchor Under Sail

You can also dig in the main bow anchor under sail (a shown in Figure 3.19), but lay out more rode before ma ing fast (Figure 3.21). When the boat has spun aroun

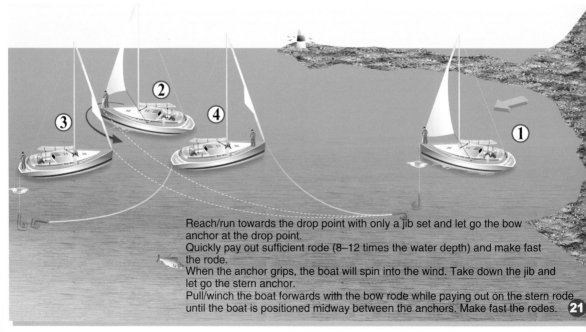

Reach/run towards the drop point with only a jib set and let go the bow anchor at the drop point.

Quickly pay out sufficient rode (8–12 times the water depth) and make fast the rode.

When the anchor grips, the boat will spin into the wind. Take down the jib and let go the stern anchor.

Pull/winch the boat forwards with the bow rode while paying out on the stern rode until the boat is positioned midway between the anchors. Make fast the rodes.

21

You should use *both a bow and a stern anchor* when you want to prevent the boat from turning, for example in a narrow river or a canal where there is a *significant tidal range*. When anchoring at *low tide* you have to let out rodes with *extra scope* and tighten them well. When the water rises, the tight rodes will dig in both anchors. As the tide ebbs again, take in on the rodes in order to keep the boat from turning too much, and then let out on the lines when the water rises again. When anchoring at *high tide* you also let out extra scope and then tighten the lines as the tide ebbs. When the water rises again, both anchors will dig in. *NB! Strong sidewinds may put a very high load on the anchors, so you should use this method with caution.*

High tide

Low tide

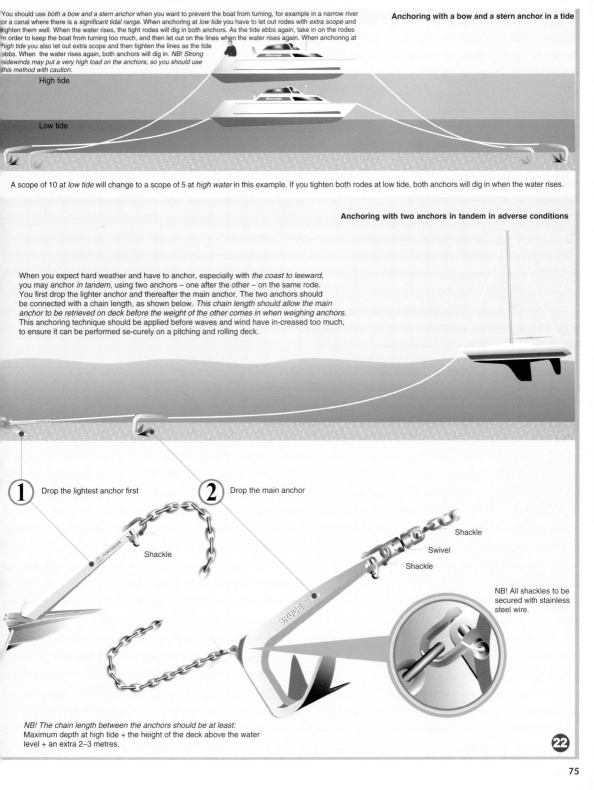

A scope of 10 at *low tide* will change to a scope of 5 at *high water* in this example. If you tighten both rodes at low tide, both anchors will dig in when the water rises.

Anchoring with two anchors in tandem in adverse conditions

When you expect hard weather and have to anchor, especially with *the coast to leeward*, you may anchor *in tandem*, using two anchors – one after the other – on the same rode. You first drop the lighter anchor and thereafter the main anchor. The two anchors should be connected with a chain length, as shown below. *This chain length should allow the main anchor to be retrieved on deck before the weight of the other comes in when weighing anchors.* This anchoring technique should be applied before waves and wind have in-creased too much, to ensure it can be performed se-curely on a pitching and rolling deck.

(1) Drop the lightest anchor first

(2) Drop the main anchor

Shackle

Shackle

Swivel

Shackle

NB! All shackles to be secured with stainless steel wire.

NB! The chain length between the anchors should be at least: Maximum depth at high tide + the height of the deck above the water level + an extra 2–3 metres.

22

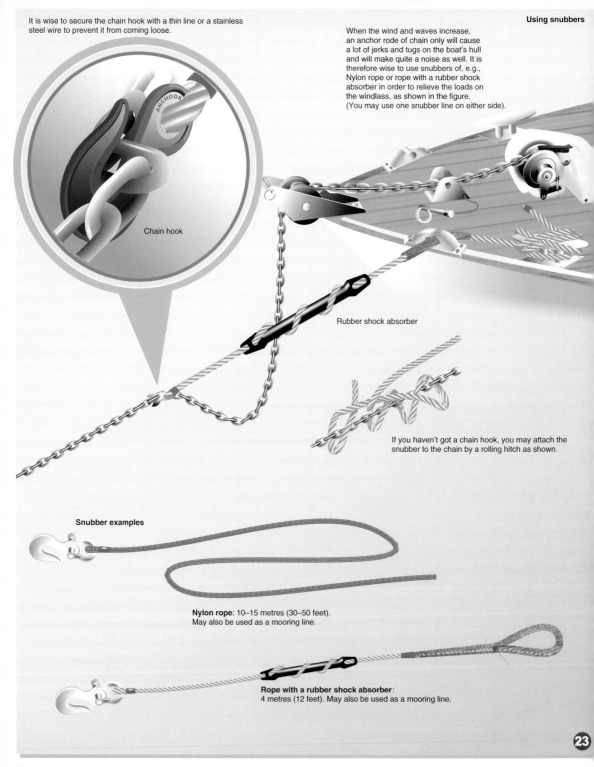

It is wise to secure the chain hook with a thin line or a stainless steel wire to prevent it from coming loose.

When the wind and waves increase, an anchor rode of chain only will cause a lot of jerks and tugs on the boat's hull and will make quite a noise as well. It is therefore wise to use snubbers of, e.g., Nylon rope or rope with a rubber shock absorber in order to relieve the loads on the windlass, as shown in the figure. (You may use one snubber line on either side.)

Chain hook

Rubber shock absorber

If you haven't got a chain hook, you may attach the snubber to the chain by a rolling hitch as shown.

Snubber examples

Nylon rope: 10–15 metres (30–50 feet). May also be used as a mooring line.

Rope with a rubber shock absorber: 4 metres (12 feet). May also be used as a mooring line.

23

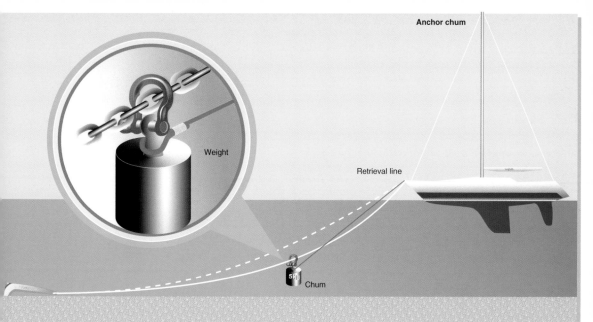

Anchor chum

Weight

Retrieval line

5kg Chum

chum is very useful for long-distance cruisers, although it should be used by all sailors. It consists of a *chain rider* (a shackle, pulley or a dedicated device) with a *weight* attached that may slide down e rode. You may make your own arrangement, as long as it is possible to retrieve the system. *A weight lowered down along the rode to approximately half the water depth will make a much better angle f pull on the anchor. It will also dampen jerks on the hull, especially with an all-chain rode.*

he load on the ground tackle increases dramatically when the waves build up. A combination of very elastic Nylon rope and chain will dampen the jerks considerably. All the same, the use of a chum is ecommended, especially with an all-chain rode. You may then anchor with much less scope and reduced swinging room. Note that when anchoring in deep waters, the weight of the ground tackle that ou have to pull in may be very high. *For long-distance cruisers, a rode of braided Nylon rope and chain used together with a good chum is an ideal solution.*

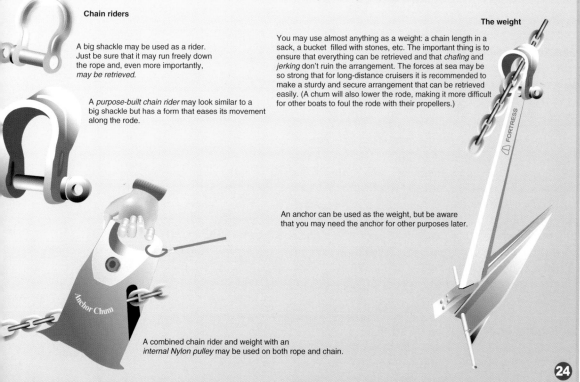

Chain riders

A big shackle may be used as a rider. Just be sure that it may run freely down the rope and, even more importantly, *may be retrieved.*

A *purpose-built chain rider* may look similar to a big shackle but has a form that eases its movement along the rode.

A combined chain rider and weight with an *internal Nylon pulley* may be used on both rope and chain.

The weight

You may use almost anything as a weight: a chain length in a sack, a bucket filled with stones, etc. The important thing is to ensure that everything can be retrieved and that *chafing* and *jerking* don't ruin the arrangement. The forces at sea may be so strong that for long-distance cruisers it is recommended to make a sturdy and secure arrangement that can be retrieved easily. (A chum will also lower the rode, making it more difficult for other boats to foul the rode with their propellers.)

An anchor can be used as the weight, but be aware that you may need the anchor for other purposes later.

FORTRESS

24

into the wind, let the *stern anchor* go (3). Pull/winch the boat forwards while paying out on the stern rode until the boat is positioned midway between the anchors (4). *This will ensure that the main anchor will dig in better and you have more control over where the boat will be positioned.*

Without a windlass it can be hard to pull the boat forwards in windy conditions. You may, however, use a *genoa* or *halyard winch*, as shown later in Figure 3.29.

With a *dominating current*, as in Figure 3.17, sail up to the drop point and let go the bow anchor. Let the boat drift astern with the current and let go the stern anchor.

WEIGHING ANCHOR

When *weighing* (taking in) the anchor, you have to apply a vertical upwards force on the anchor to break it loose. Position the boat close to the anchor and break it loose one way or another. *Always have a broom and bucket ready as the rode is pulled in!*

Weighing anchor *with a windlass* is normally quite simple. You winch in the rode while cleaning the rope, chain and anchor of mud and seaweed. Use the boat's engine at low forward speed to get the boat up to the anchor position, taking in the rode as you go. The windlass is normally capable of breaking loose the anchor and lifting it up to the bow rollers. With a *manual windlass* it may be wise to use hands to pull in the rode and only use the windlass to break loose the anchor.

Weighing anchor *without a windlass* can be heavy work and it is very important that the crew member(s) weighing the anchor take care of their backs! Normally, a person in reasonably good shape may weigh an anchor manually on boats of less than 40 feet with proper use of the engine. If it is impossible to break loose the anchor with bare hands (or a winch), you can follow the procedures shown in Figures 3.25, 3.26 and 3.27. If these don't work, the anchor is probably tangled up in some old chain or debris on the seabed or is jammed in rocks. In such cases an anchor buoy will be of great help (see Figure 3.14).

Weighing Anchor Under Sail

You should always carry enough sails to manoeuvre safely when breaking loose the anchor under sail. Different types of boat and different crews demand different

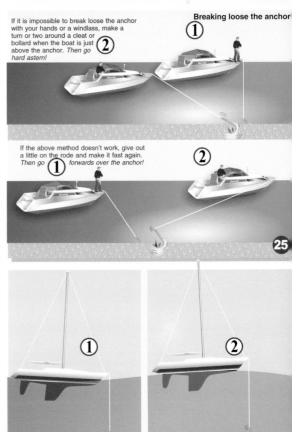

If it is impossible to break loose the anchor with your hands or a windlass, make a turn or two around a cleat or bollard when the boat is just ② above the anchor. *Then go* ① *hard astern!*

Breaking loose the anchor

①

If the above method doesn't work, give out a little on the rode and make it fast again. *Then go* ① *forwards over the anchor!*

②

25

①   ②

Make a turn or two around a bollard or cleat with the rode tight when the boat is just above the anchor and down in the *trough of a wave*.

The next wave crest will lift the boat and break loose the anchor. You use the boat as leverage. *NB! Be cautious with this method. In a rough sea, a cleat may easily be ripped off!*

26

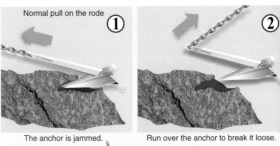

Normal pull on the rode ①

②

The anchor is jammed.

Run over the anchor to break it loose.

The Sarca anchor lets the shackle slide in a *slot* in the anchor shank so the anchor may be broken loose.

27

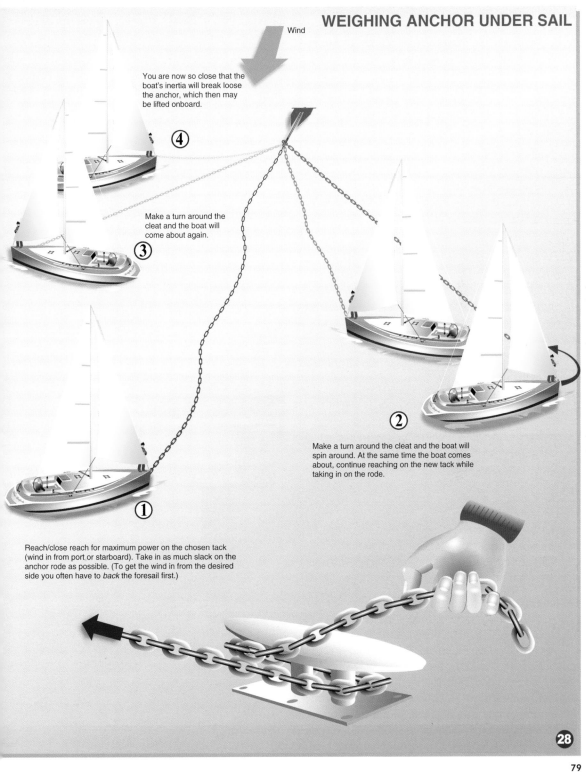

Wind

You are now so close that the boat's inertia will break loose the anchor, which then may be lifted onboard.

④

Make a turn around the cleat and the boat will come about again.

③

②

Make a turn around the cleat and the boat will spin around. At the same time the boat comes about, continue reaching on the new tack while taking in on the rode.

①

Reach/close reach for maximum power on the chosen tack (wind in from port or starboard). Take in as much slack on the anchor rode as possible. (To get the wind in from the desired side you often have to *back* the foresail first.)

28

sail settings to handle the boat. If current is dominating and there is enough room, you can weigh anchor and let the boat drift with the current until you can set a foresail. You later luff and hoist the main.

Weighing anchor under sail *using a windlass* implies that you can hoist the main and winch the boat up to the anchor location as long as the wind is more or less on the bow.

Weighing anchor under sail *without the use of a windlass* in light or moderate winds also makes it possible to hoist the main and pull the boat up to the anchor position. In stronger winds you may try to sail up to the anchor, as shown in Figure 3.28.

Generally, you should use engine or sail power when possible in order to protect your back (unless you consider it good physical exercise) and a windlass where possible. In any case it is wise to try out the various techniques, as you may need them later under conditions where it will be impossible to use your hands only.

It is very important that you let the boat itself do most of the work when pulling up the anchor. Don't pull wildly on the rode but make a good grip and lean backwards, waiting for the boat to start moving. Then continue pulling evenly in this manner. It becomes easier as the boat gains speed. When the boat is almost straight above the anchor, make a turn around the bollard or cleat. Normally, the anchor will then break loose.

If the anchor has been fouled at the seabed you may try to power around it with the rode quite tight. Try to pull hard in various directions. If the anchor moves a little but doesn't break loose completely, it may be fouled in an old chain or rope on the seabed. Try to tighten the rode as much as possible and let it go suddenly. The anchor will then often break loose.

On a sailing yacht without a windlass, you may use a *genoa* or *halyard winch* to weigh the anchor when it becomes heavy (Figure 3.29). You can use a *chain hook* or a *rolling hitch* (see Figure 3.23) to attach a line to the rode. Lead this line to a genoa or halyard winch (using snatch blocks if necessary). Winch in a bit on the rode and lock it with a *chain stopper* or *pawl*. Then attach the chain hook to the rode as close to the bow rollers as possible and winch in more of the rode. (If the rode is rope, the rolling hitch has to be loosened up and pushed

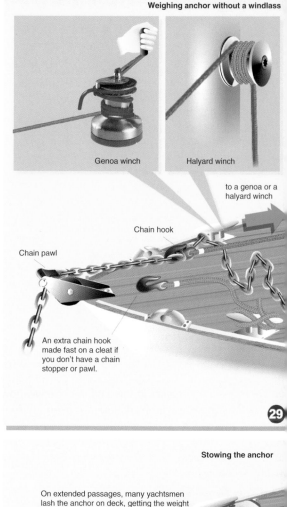

Weighing anchor without a windlass

Genoa winch

Halyard winch

to a genoa or a halyard winch

Chain hook

Chain pawl

An extra chain hook made fast on a cleat if you don't have a chain stopper or pawl.

29

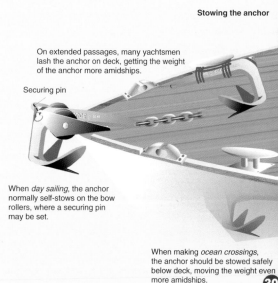

Stowing the anchor

On extended passages, many yachtsmen lash the anchor on deck, getting the weight of the anchor more amidships.

Securing pin

When *day sailing*, the anchor normally self-stows on the bow rollers, where a securing pin may be set.

When making *ocean crossings*, the anchor should be stowed safely below deck, moving the weight even more amidships.

30

urther down the rode and tightened before you can winch in more of the rode.)

It is very important that you make a good arrangement for your ground tackle that works well even in hard weather, not least to save your back. Also, be very cautious when handling chain. Try to make permanent rules regarding how to handle your gear and always brief the crew thoroughly on these rules prior to anchoring.

Stowing the Anchors

Many anchors self-stow very well in the bow rollers when they come up (Figure 3.30). The securing pin should be inserted – the anchor will be ready to be dropped at short notice even with the pin inserted.

Note that a weight that far forward is not very advantageous for a yacht, especially not for a modern, light sailing yacht. Therefore, it is wise to move the anchor further aft on extended passages or stow it below deck when crossing oceans or open seas, although many modern yachts are designed to sail with the anchor permanently stowed in the bow rollers.

USING TWO BOW ANCHORS

The use of a bow anchor together with a stern anchor has been described earlier in this chapter. We will now take a look at how two bow anchors are used in order to reduce the boat's turning circle in confined spaces with big shifts in wind and currents (Figures 3.31 and 3.32). They can also be used to secure the boat in rough weather while still enabling it to swing to wind and current. Periodically one of the anchors takes the whole load and sometimes the load is distributed across both anchors.

The anchors may be laid out at a maximum angle of 60° in relation to each other. In light weather, where you are aiming to reduce the turning circle as much as possible, greater angles can be used. At an angle between the anchors of 60°, the pull on each rode is approximately 60% of the total force to keep the boat in place, as shown in Figure 3.33. With an angle of 120° between the anchors, the pull on each rode will be equal to the total force (100%).

Note that the pull on each rode increases strongly when the angle between the anchors is increased! With an angle of 180° between the anchors, the pull on each rode

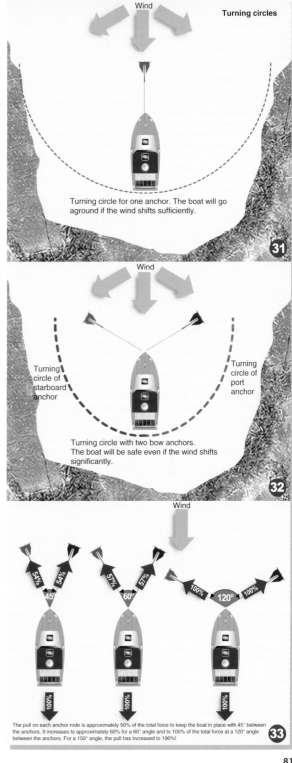

Turning circles

Turning circle for one anchor. The boat will go aground if the wind shifts sufficiently.

31

Wind

Turning circle of starboard anchor

Turning circle of port anchor

Turning circle with two bow anchors. The boat will be safe even if the wind shifts significantly.

32

Wind

54% 54% 45%

57% 57% 60%

100% 120° 100%

100% 100% 100%

The pull on each anchor rode is approximately 50% of the total force to keep the boat in place with 45° between the anchors. It increases to approximately 60% for a 60° angle and to 100% of the total force at a 120° angle between the anchors. For a 150° angle, the pull has increased to 190%!

33

will, theoretically, be infinite with the wind abeam. In this case the anchors will probably break loose with no guarantee that they will ever dig in again.

However, anchoring with an angle between the anchors of 180° is being used in confined spaces where *tidal currents are dominating* in weak or moderate winds (as was shown in Figure 3.17). If you choose to use *two bow anchors*, you may apply the same technique to dig in the anchors. *Note, you should never anchor in this manner if strong winds abeam can be expected!*

Anchoring with an angle between the anchors of approximately 180° is used a lot in the USA and the Caribbean, where it is referred to as a *Bahamian moor*. This anchoring method should be used with caution.When anchoring for really *adverse conditions*, the angle between the anchors should not be greater than 60°. Then, the pull on each rode will be approximately 60% of the total force when equally loaded.

Whatever the angle is between the anchors, each anchor has to take the whole load alone if the wind shifts enough. It is therefore important that both anchors have enough holding power to take the whole load alone.

The two bow anchor rodes may be made fast on separate cleats or bollards, making it easy to adjust each rode. However, often the second anchor rode is shackled to the main anchor rode and the connection is lowered down below the keel of the boat, so it may swing freely (see Figure 3.35).

It is important that the anchors are laid out in such an order that you avoid, as far as possible, any possibility that one anchor rode will cross the other when the wind shifts. Big wind shifts occur when a *cold front* or a *thunder cloud* passes or when the *sea breeze* dies in the evening and the *land breeze* starts to blow in the opposite direction.

Two Bow Anchors with an Angle of 150–180° Between Them

When anchoring in a confined space with a *tidal current*, the so-called Bahamian moor is used, especially in the US and the Caribbean (Figure 3.34(a)). Here, you first go upstream and drop the *first bow anchor* at the desired location. Motor or let the boat drift slowly astern while paying out sufficient rode and then dig in the anchor.

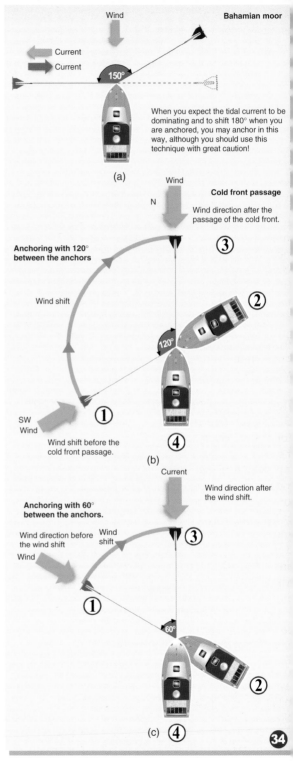

Wind

Bahamian moor

Current

Current

150°

When you expect the tidal current to be dominating and to shift 180° when you are anchored, you may anchor in this way, although you should use this technique with great caution!

(a)

Wind

N

Cold front passage

Wind direction after the passage of the cold front.

③

Anchoring with 120° between the anchors

Wind shift

②

120°

①

SW Wind

Wind shift before the cold front passage.

④

(b)

Current

Wind direction after the wind shift.

Anchoring with 60° between the anchors.

Wind direction before the wind shift

Wind shift

③

Wind

①

60°

②

(c) ④

34

Motor or drift slowly further astern until you have twice as much scope as normal, then drop the *second bow anchor*. Now motor or pull the boat back while you take in on the first and pay out on the second rode until the boat is midway between the anchors. Then carefully dig in the second anchor. Tighten both rodes well.

This method works best if a moderate wind is blowing across the current, keeping the boat on the same side of the straight line between the anchors. *The method has an apparent weakness if there is a strong wind blowing across the current, making both anchors vulnerable to breaking loose.*

In normal conditions with moderate to fresh winds, you may set the anchors with an angle of 120° between them when a great wind shift is expected and you want to reduce the boat's turning circle. One of the anchors may be a kedge, but in more adverse conditions *both anchors should have enough holding power to take the whole load alone.*

When a cold front passes (in the northern hemisphere), a shift in the wind of up to 120° occurs. The northerly winds after such a passage may be very strong!

Two Bow Anchors with an Angle of 120° Between Them

For this configuration, go against the wind and drop the *port anchor* at the desired location (Figure 3.34(b) (1)). Motor or drift slowly astern, paying out sufficient rode, and dig in the anchor properly (2). Then motor forwards at a course approximately 120° to starboard of the course you had when dropping the first anchor and pay out on the port rode until you have made a distance at least as long as for the port anchor. Now drop the starboard anchor (3) and motor straight astern while paying out sufficient starboard rode and taking in on the port rode. Then make fast both rodes and dig in the starboard anchor (4) by going hard astern. *Always be very cautious not to get the rodes caught in the propeller when laying out two anchors.*

In adverse conditions many yachtsmen advocate either laying two anchors with an angle of 45° between them or in tandem (Figure 3.22). Others are in favour of using *one big anchor* with good holding power. *The problem with the latter, however, is that when the wind shifts significantly, a single anchor may break loose without resetting.*

Bruce, CQR and Delta anchors will often reset well on a sand or mud bottom after breaking loose. On harder bottoms they are not as likely to reset well.

There are many firm opinions on how to anchor, and many of them are contradictory! In this book I have tried to describe some principles that are generally accepted by the sailing community. *The most important thing is to gain your own experience with your own boat and ground tackle. Try out your gear and the various techniques described in calm weather so you will be well prepared for adverse conditions.*

Anchoring With Two Bow Anchors

Here, you use much the same technique as shown in Figure 3.17. Always be cautious to avoid getting the rodes caught in the propeller! If in doubt, set the engine in neutral until you know where the rode is. You can also set a course that excludes the possibility of getting the rode caught in the propeller. The problem comes when motoring astern from positions 3–4 in Figure 3.36. You can avoid the problem by setting the engine in neutral and letting the wind blow you astern. Equally, the crew may keep an eye on the starboard rode while you motor astern.

Digging in Two Bow Anchors Under Sail

This is a variation on the technique shown in Figure 3.21. You reach and spin the boat to *starboard* when making fast the *starboard anchor rode* (take in the foresail or let go the sheet just before making fast the rode). The *port anchor* is dropped when the boat exposes its port side to the wind and then the same length is let out on the port anchor rode as for the starboard one, while the wind pushes the boat astern. Make fast the port rode (Figure 3.37). The starboard anchor will most likely dig in better than the port one because of the higher boat speed when forced to stop. You may now shackle one rode to the other and lower the connection point below the keel, so the boat may swing freely. If you expect swell or adverse conditions, you should rig snubbing lines.

USING A DINGHY

Sooner or later you will have to row or motor out an anchor using a *dinghy* (Figure 3.38). This may be when you need to lay out a *second* or a *third* anchor when you expect adverse conditions or to keep the boat off a

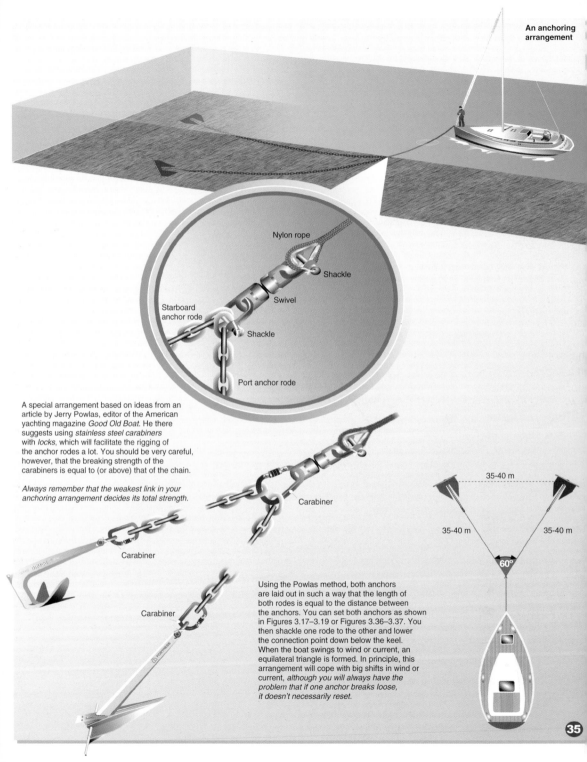

An anchoring arrangement

Nylon rope

Shackle

Swivel

Starboard anchor rode

Shackle

Port anchor rode

A special arrangement based on ideas from an article by Jerry Powlas, editor of the American yachting magazine *Good Old Boat*. He there suggests using *stainless steel carabiners* with *locks*, which will facilitate the rigging of the anchor rodes a lot. You should be very careful, however, that the breaking strength of the carabiners is equal to (or above) that of the chain.

Always remember that the weakest link in your anchoring arrangement decides its total strength.

Carabiner

Carabiner

Carabiner

35-40 m

35-40 m

35-40 m

60°

Using the Powlas method, both anchors are laid out in such a way that the length of both rodes is equal to the distance between the anchors. You can set both anchors as shown in Figures 3.17–3.19 or Figures 3.36–3.37. You then shackle one rode to the other and lower the connection point down below the keel. When the boat swings to wind or current, an equilateral triangle is formed. In principle, this arrangement will cope with big shifts in wind or current, *although you will always have the problem that if one anchor breaks loose, it doesn't necessarily reset.*

35

ANCHORING WITH TWO BOW ANCHORS

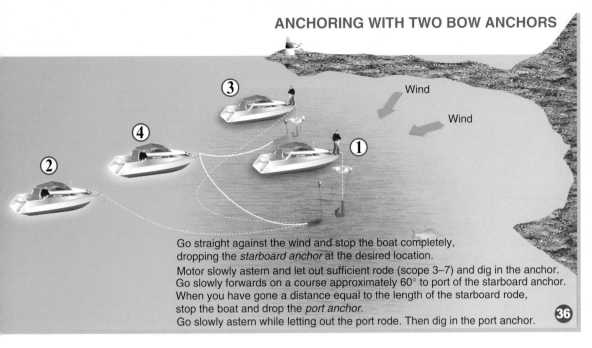

Wind

Wind

Go straight against the wind and stop the boat completely,
dropping the *starboard anchor* at the desired location.
Motor slowly astern and let out sufficient rode (scope 3–7) and dig in the anchor.
Go slowly forwards on a course approximately 60° to port of the starboard anchor.
When you have gone a distance equal to the length of the starboard rode,
stop the boat and drop the *port anchor*.
Go slowly astern while letting out the port rode. Then dig in the port anchor.

36

hallow. It may also be to enable you *to warp* the boat
ff a shallow after *grounding*. It is therefore important to
now some basic techniques. *Primarily, you should never*
y to row out the anchor while towing the rode along the *seabed. This way you will never reach the desired drop location!* You should also note that it is important to carry 10–20% more rode than the depth indicates, due to the difficulties of laying the rode straight.

DIGGING IN TWO BOW ANCHORS UNDER SAIL

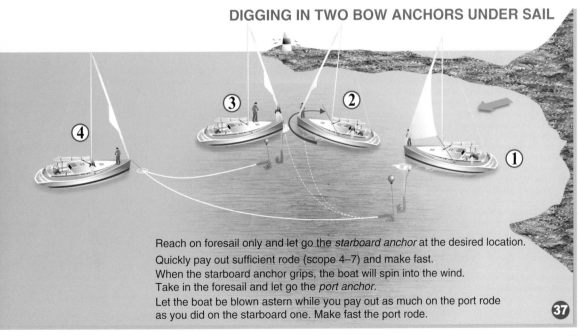

Reach on foresail only and let go the *starboard anchor* at the desired location.
Quickly pay out sufficient rode (scope 4–7) and make fast.
When the starboard anchor grips, the boat will spin into the wind.
Take in the foresail and let go the *port anchor*.
Let the boat be blown astern while you pay out as much on the port rode
as you did on the starboard one. Make fast the port rode.

37

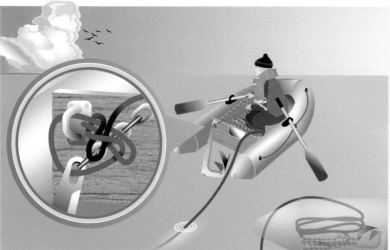

With a chain-only rode it will be difficult, if not impossible, to row out the anchor in a dinghy in adverse conditions. Therefore, a *third anchor/ warp anchor* should have a rope rode with a few metres of chain near the anchor (a warp anchor is used to pull the boat loose when aground or when the boat is to be moved without engine or sail). The pull from the rode as it is laid out will force the dinghy to swing a lot, especially in strong winds. *Go slowly, keeping an eye on the rode, especially if it is chain only*. Watch out to avoid the rode being fouled on anything, including arms, legs, engine controls or the fuel tank! A stainless steel or plastic *mounting* on the stern over which the rode may slide and a *rubber mat* to protect the dinghy's bottom will be wise.

First place the anchor on the dinghy's bottom or suspend it from the stern using a *slip knot*, as shown. Lay sufficient rode in nice loops, ensuring that the rode will run freely out behind the dinghy while rowing or motoring ahead. When you reach the desired location and have paid out most of the rode, untie the knot and let the anchor sink down to the bottom.

38

USING A BOW OR STERN ANCHOR AND MOORING LINE ASHORE

Mooring with the *bow to a rock or quay* with a *stern anchor* is common in Scandinavia and is often called a *Scandinavian moor* (Figure 3.39(a)). You should always drop the anchor far enough away from shore in order to obtain adequate holding power and then continue towards the rock or quay, where the crew fastens the bow. Then you should carefully try to dig in the anchor by motoring or using a winch in order to be moored safely.

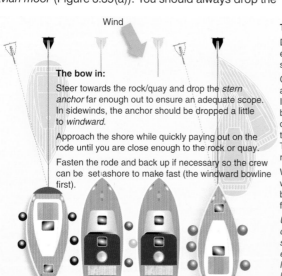

Wind

The bow in:

Steer towards the rock/quay and drop the *stern anchor* far enough out to ensure an adequate scope. In sidewinds, the anchor should be dropped a little to *windward*.

Approach the shore while quickly paying out on the rode until you are close enough to the rock or quay.

Fasten the rode and back up if necessary so the crew can be set ashore to make fast (the windward bowline first).

Bow in

The stern in:

Drop the *bow anchor* sufficiently far enough out to ensure adequate scope. In sidewinds, the anchor should be dropped a little to *windward*.

Go astern as soon as the anchor hits the bottom and *keep good speed* while paying out on the rode. If the bow blows off the wind, you may try to hold back a little on the rode to straighten the boat. If this doesn't help, set the engine in full forward and put the helm over to get the bow into the wind again. Then continue going astern while paying out on the rode.

When close enough, fasten the rode and go *forwards* with the engine if necessary so the crew may be set ashore to make fast the stern (windward line first).

Use all the fenders onboard. Don't take any chances on acrobatic jumps ashore. It is good seamanship to stop and try again if you encounter problems. In the night or when you leave the boat, you should tighten the anchor line, pulling the boat further out from shore. This will prevent it from bumping against rocks or the quay.

Stern in

It is often easier to turn around and look astern when going astern. Practise this!

39

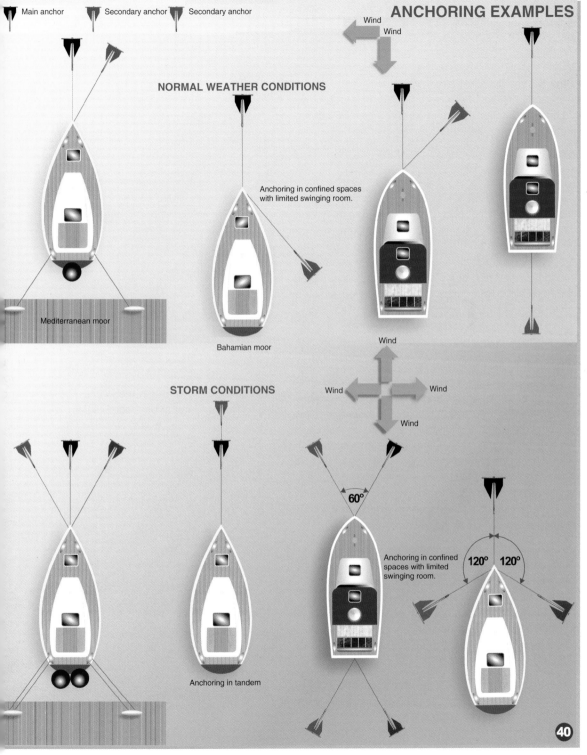

Main anchor   Secondary anchor   Secondary anchor

Wind
Wind

NORMAL WEATHER CONDITIONS

Anchoring in confined spaces
with limited swinging room.

Mediterranean moor

Bahamian moor

Wind

STORM CONDITIONS

Wind   Wind

Wind

60°

Anchoring in confined
spaces with limited
swinging room.

120°   120°

Anchoring in tandem

40

87

Mooring with the *stern to a rock or quay* with a *bow anchor* is more complicated and is called a *Mediterranean moor* (Figure 3.39(b)). Here, you drop the anchor far enough out to obtain an adequate scope, a little to *windward* in sidewinds, and start going astern as soon as the anchor hits the bottom. Maintain a *good speed astern* to keep the boat steerable. When moored, try to dig in the anchor using the windlass or by motoring carefully astern.

MISCELLANY

Hand Signals

It is very important that everybody has agreed on how to communicate during anchoring. The helmsman's position is normally far from the crew, and noise from wind, sea and the engine makes it difficult to hear even when shouting. *Many unlucky incidents and accidents could have been avoided with better communication onboard yachts*. It doesn't matter which signals you use as long as they are unambiguous and easily understood. *The most important thing is to set up a system that is used consistently onboard (and may also be used when mooring)*.

Figure 3.41 shows a simple system for communication between the helmsman and the crew on the foredeck. *Use this, or parts of it, when making your own system*. What is to be communicated and to whom depends on the boat's size, gear and organization. For example, the water depth is important to the crew at the bow so that they know how much rode to pay out. When weighing anchor, the helmsman will want to know the exact direction to the anchor. The crew can see this more easily by watching the rode and then pointing it out to the helmsman.

It is also important that the helmsman knows when the anchor has *broken loose from the seabed*, because the boat then drifts freely and has to be manoeuvred away from other boats and obstacles. When the anchor is *out of the water*, a crew member may extend an arm, forming an OK sign with the thumb and index finger. The boat may now be manoeuvred without risk of fouling the rode in the propeller.

These are, as mentioned earlier, only proposed signals. If you wish, make your own signals, as long as they are consistent and used systematically.

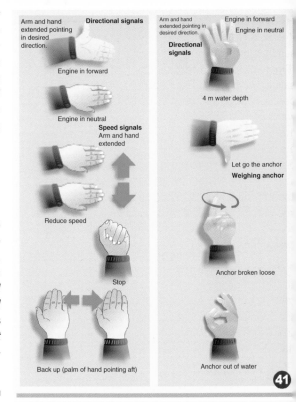

Arm and hand extended pointing in desired direction.

Directional signals

Engine in forward

Engine in neutral

Speed signals
Arm and hand extended

Reduce speed

Stop

Back up (palm of hand pointing aft)

Arm and hand extended pointing in desired direction.

Engine in forward

Engine in neutral

Directional signals

4 m water depth

Let go the anchor

Weighing anchor

Anchor broken loose

Anchor out of water

(41)

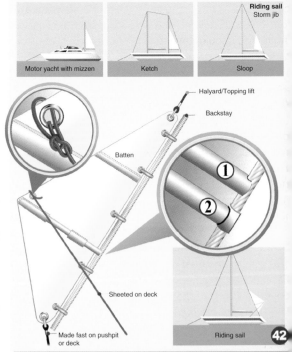

Motor yacht with mizzen

Ketch

Sloop

Riding sail
Storm jib

Halyard/Topping lift

Backstay

Batten

(1)

(2)

Sheeted on deck

Made fast on pushpit or deck

Riding sail

(42)

Riding Sails

If your boat has a tendency to 'sail at anchor', a *riding sail* that turns the boat into a *windvane* can be a solution (Figure 3.42). The reason why many boats (especially sailing yachts) sail back and forth at anchor is that the *centre of effort* (windage) of topsides and rig is well forward of the *underwater centre of lateral resistance*, i.e. the point that the boat turns around. A gust of wind or a small change in the wind direction will make the bow bear away until the wind is almost abeam. The boat then sails away until the rode stops it. This process repeats itself all the time both to port and to starboard. *It is very uncomfortable and, in a confined space, may cause a collision with another boat 'out of phase'. In addition, the jerks on the rode may break loose the anchor.*

With a riding sail at the stern, the centre of effort moves aft and reduces the boat's (both motor and sailing yachts) tendency to 'sail at anchor', keeping the boat head to wind. Boats with a mizzen may use this reefed down, or a storm jib may be hanked on to the backstay, as shown in Figure 3.42. A better solution still is to make a purpose-built riding sail – a flat cut of heavy cloth with hollow foot and leech to reduce flutter. Full-length battens will reduce the flutter even more. GRP or aluminium tubing may be used to keep the clew out away from the backstay, pointing aft away from the cockpit. The tubing should have a slot (1) or another form (2) in the end, preventing it from sliding off the backstay.

Laying Out an Anchor Abeam (Breton Moor)

If a strong wind is blowing on to the quay and there is some swell, it may be necessary to row or motor out an anchor that can keep the boat away from the quay or rock (Figure 3.43). You have to get the anchor far enough out to get enough holding power. At the same time, you have to ensure that no other boats will try to moor alongside your boat.

Anchoring From the Stern

If you anchor the boat with only a stern anchor, a similar effect to that obtained when using a riding sail can be achieved. *But you should never anchor from the stern alone for anything but short periods in very light winds and calm seas, because this could cause the boat to be swamped or capsized!*

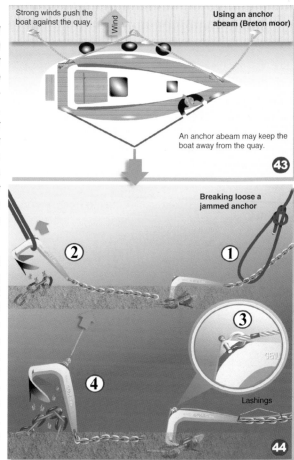

Strong winds push the boat against the quay.

Wind

Using an anchor abeam (Breton moor)

An anchor abeam may keep the boat away from the quay.

43

Breaking loose a jammed anchor

② ①

③

④

Lashings

44

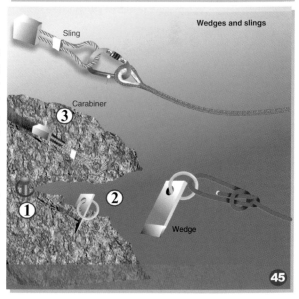

Wedges and slings

Sling

Carabiner

③

① ②

Wedge

45

Breaking Loose a Jammed Anchor

If the anchor is jammed on the seabed you may, in addition to the methods described earlier, also try the following:

1. Take in as much as possible on the rode and make fast.

2. Make a big loop of a length of chain or a strong line around the rode and send it down the rode. If using rope, you must attach a weight, for example a heavy shackle, to the loop in order to make it slide down the rode (Figure 3.44(1)).

3. Pay out a bit on the rode and then try to run over the anchor in the opposite direction to the rode. The loop will now be pulled up the anchor shank (2) and the anchor can be lifted up and away from whatever had fouled it.

Another method of avoiding problems with a jammed anchor is to use a *tripline*. This line is attached to the *anchor crown* (3) and fastened with *tape* or *twine* along the rode. The tripline must be long enough to make it possible to retrieve the end and lead it to a winch, even at high tide. If the anchor is jammed, you only winch in on the tripline. The tape or twine will break and the anchor will lift up from the crown and hopefully come loose (4).

Mooring to Rocks

In Scandinavia it is common to moor the *bow to a rock* with a *stern anchor* set, or even moor along the rock with lines ashore and a lot of fenders out. *Mooring rings* (Figure 3.45(1)) can be found in some places, although you often have to use *wedges* hammered down into cracks in the rock (2). These wedges are often big and heavy and demand hammering down to sit well. In addition, they may cause damage by breaking loose pieces of the rock.

A better solution is to use so-called *slings*, as used by mountain climbers (3). These slings are light and strong and can be easily fastened in small crevices in the rock without any tools. *Carabiners* attached to *mooring lines* can be clipped on to the slings, making a quick and safe mooring.

On the whole, much *mountaineering equipment* is worth taking a look at for yachtsmen. The equipment is light and very strong and usually very easy to use. The only problem is that you have to check any light alloys regularly for signs of *corrosion*.

SUMMARY

1. Select a *well-sheltered anchorage* with ample *swinging room*.

2. Check the *depth* and *bottom conditions* by circling around the desired anchor location *making soundings*.

3. Select your *anchoring method* and *scope*. You often have to use the same as any adjacent boats. Ask them!

4. Remember that various boats *behave differently at anchor* (even in dying winds).

5. Approach the desired drop point slowly, *bow to wind or current*, and stop the boat completely.

6. When the boat just starts to move astern (by engine, wind or current), *quickly lower the anchor to the bottom* and then *slowly pay out the rode* as the boat drifts or motors back, thus avoiding the chain piling up and fouling the anchor. Ensure that the rode is not too tight, making the anchor drag.

7. If the bow bears away due to the wind, hold back on the rode from time to time to straighten the bow. When you have paid out a scope of approximately 3, make fast the rode, so the anchor *starts to dig in*. Then continue backing and pay out the rode until the decided scope (5–10) has been obtained.

8. Make fast the rode again. Motor slowly astern to let the *anchor dig in properly*. Increase the revs to almost maximum if you are staying overnight. How much power you should use depends on the seabed conditions. With mud it may be wise to let the wind do the job. Under normal conditions, 2000 revs may be sufficient. If you expect adverse conditions, use maximum revs.

9. Use objects ashore (trees, houses, rocks, towers, etc.), preferably abeam, to check that the boat no longer moves astern. Then the anchor is firmly set. Make this check from time to time. You can feel a dragging anchor by setting your foot on or holding the rode and feeling the jerks as it bumps along the seabed. A well-set anchor will not shake the rode. If this does happen, you have to pay out more rode and repeat points 8 and 9. If it still drags, take in the rode and anchor and start the whole process over again.

With waves or swell in a different direction to the current, it may be wise to rig a spring line from the rode to a cleat or winch aft as shown. The boat will roll less with the bow head to the waves, making it a lot more comfortable onboard.

'Flat calm or force 10. I always wear one.'

Whether they're training or out on a shout, RNLI crew members always wear lifejackets. It's a rule informed by years of experience. They know that, whatever the weather, the sea's extremely unpredictable – and can turn at a moment's notice. They see people caught out all the time. People who've risked, or even lost their lives as a result. The fact is, a lifejacket will buy you vital time in the water – and could even save your life. But only if you're wearing it.

For advice on choosing a lifejacket and how to wear it correctly, call us on 0800 328 0600 (UK) or 1800 789 589 (RoI) or visit our website rnli.org.uk/seasafety/lifejackets

LIFEJACKETS

Useless unless worn